The Depressed Millennial:
Surviving Unmet Expectations

First Printing, 2018

ISBN-13: 978-1718605824
ISBN-10: 171860582X

Create Space Independent Publishing Company
4900 La Cross Rd.
North Charleston, SC 29406

www.createspace.com

Dedication

To my son: Dacari J. Middlebrooks, II. My prayer for you is that the things I've struggled with—you will hurdle over. No father could be prouder of a son than I am of you. Your presence in this world has made my life better.

To Lauren: May your witness give strength to wives who deal with depressed spouses all over the world. I am forever grateful for your support, love, and sincerity. I'm not sure if I would have made it this far without you.

Millennials Share Their Truth

I have come to find that happiness is not something that you stumble upon getting out of bed in the morning. It is a robust and daily effort comprised of rituals that are both personal and rewarding. It is learning how to redirect your brain to replace the negative with positive. Just like an athlete trains his muscles, I train my mind and happiness is not a spectator sport. Wanna fight depression? Make a list of who you want to be and *practice* being that person every day.

- *Destiny Stoke*
Creative Director of Ateaelle

My battle with depression is an on-going battle. It's a daily thing that comes and goes, however, I use optimism as a source of strength. I believe that good things happen to those who remain positive. One of the ways I fight depression is being active at work, and in the gym. The gym is my safe haven in the midst of darkness.

- *Tay Hawes*
CEO of Kick Me Enterprises

I'm a depression awareness advocate and author of the book, "If You Are Reading This, You Survived." I am surviving because I acknowledged and owned that I suffered with depression. My healing techniques have included raising awareness of this mental disease, helping others by sharing my experiences and letting them know that I, too, am fighting with them.

-Kimberly Garrett
Author of "If You Are Reading This, You Survived"
CEO of Faithful August Foundation

Foreword
Dr. Joseph Warren Walker, III

Life is filled with inevitabilities and uncertainties that challenge the best of us in ways we never imagined. The human tendency is to mask our pain and function at high levels publicly while crashing privately. One of the most powerful signpost of our maturity is when we embrace the critical space of self-reflection. It's there that our truth meets us face on and we are forced to deal with it or accept the fact that it will deal with us. It takes incredible courage to be honest amidst public perception and scrutiny. When we are willing to be so bold, we then allow our lives to be made whole as well as be used to benefit others along the way.

This book is destined to help and empower so many people. Dacari has discovered the power in sharing his story. I've had the privilege of mentoring him and watching his evolution and I know first-hand how remarkable a journey this has been for him. There are so many people who operate in ministry and other professions who have not found that safe space to be honest about depression. It is often seen as "taboo" in minority communities. It is very seldom discussed in the church because it creates for many a theological tension around instantaneous deliverance verses the necessary processes we must walk through in order to truly be free from its grip.

As a Bishop in the Lord's church for over 20 years, I've seen so much depression among leadership, yet many didn't have a safe place to discuss it. Dacari's transparency gives us all permission to begin the needed discussion around our careers and how they affect us personally each and every day. Our unmet expectations, failures, flaws and disappointments should create opportunities for us to reevaluate our lives and discover a fruitful path forward. This book will give you a point of identification and comfort knowing you are not alone in the struggle. It will also provide hope that there is a lot of life to live.

I am so proud of my mentee Dacari and I truly believe that as an African-American young man who addresses this issue head on, he has set himself apart as a leader equipped to help others be successful in their personal journey toward wholeness. As you read this book you will laugh, cry, reflect and regroup. Above all you will see the grace of God at work in the life of one young man and realize that this same grace is available for us all.

Table of Contents

Introduction
I Almost Didn't Make It: The Year of 33

It was a cool spring day, and I was hurting. I was frustrated with life. Nothing made sense anymore. I hopped in my truck, and drove to Alpharetta, GA. As I exited the freeway, I smiled, and said, "Ok, I'm ready now." See, I had prepared for this day. A few months before, I changed my life insurance policy, shared cool stories with my little brothers, and said "I love you" often to my family, and those I considered friends. Guys: on this day, I planned to commit suicide.

Suicide had been on my mind for a while. What stopped me before was the fact that I had a newborn baby. I kept fighting for him, but on this day—I was tired. I was done. Despite having a lovely wife, a beautiful son, a job, home, family—everything you could imagine, I wanted out of this life. It didn't matter anymore.

As I exited the freeway, I drove two blocks where I wanted to end it all. But before I tell you what happened next— let me share this: I planned to kill myself not far from my therapist's office. I knew the area well. I knew the exact spot. I knew I would be found quickly. I didn't want my family to look for my body all day or for days. I had it all figured out, and then....

I'd gotten off the exit and drove the two blocks, but there was a detour sign surrounding the entire area. I couldn't get through.

I was stuck. I was angry.

Yet, in that moment—I knew that God had saved me from me. I pulled over to the nearest parking lot, and wept for 30 minutes. What I discovered was a grace that was beyond me. It's what Max Lucado's idea of grace is that allowed me to know this type of grace: *The meaning of life. The wasted years of life. The poor choices of life. God answers the mess of life with one word: GRACE."* I realized that nothing I had done or ever could do will keep me from God's grace.

After experiencing this low moment, I knew I was really in trouble. I realized that I needed help. I often questioned why people committed suicide. I used to say things like, "They are so selfish!" "Don't they know people love them?" "What about their kids?" I learned, in one moment, not to judge a situation until you're in it.

I honestly think people commit suicide because of other people. I questioned my existence, my value, and if people really cared about me. I felt the weight of being a husband, father, son, brother, and friend. It was almost too much to bear. I gave so much of myself, but left many spaces empty. I would leave stages where I was applauded by thousands, and go back to my hotel room, and weep. I was sick, and I didn't see a way out, but that darn detour sign gave me a second chance! I now believe that every day you wake up, it's a reminder that God has more work for you to do.

I've battled with depression for 13 years now. I masked it by creating real life filters. I gave people the narrative I wanted them to have, and not the one they should know. In a real sense, I 'catfished' myself. I created a fictitious image and perception that made people look in awe, but in reality, I was suffering.

I've suffered significant losses along this journey. I'm extremely vulnerable and transparent about my bout with depression in this book. To those I've hurt and disconnected from--I apologize. I recognize that intentions don't substitute actions, but I couldn't see or stop myself from self-destructing. I lived through a dark lens for a long time. It became the normative gaze of how I saw things and processed life. I'm hoping this book will create a conversation around Millennial's and Mental Health (Not Exclusive to Millennial's, but I'm passionate about this group).

This book explores five different themes, or messages surrounding my depression, what caused it, and how have I survived. Part 1 deals with the loss of my best friend, questioning God, and PTSD. Part 2 invites you into the eyes and hearts of a Millennial. We define this generation, and gain a sense of clarity around how this group views faith, family, and career. Part 3 is interesting, because I open the eyes of those who want to know what it's like to work for a Pastor/CEO and mega-church. Part 4 is my most vulnerable chapter because I explore friendships, and marriage. I allow you to see what happens when you create false expectations—which leads to unmet expectations. Part 5 sums up the entire book. We look at the brain, and its functions when dealing with depression. We also see strategies on how I'm surviving depression.

Though I've shared my story, please understand I'm still surviving—I have yet to conquer depression. Every day is a journey. Every day I have to be intentional about creating a mood that sparks happiness. It's not over, I'm just beginning

Part One:

I Still Haven't Forgiven Myself

*"For running to the grave getting closer to death,
I still ain't forgave myself.
For anyone who ever wondered how I felt,
I still ain't forgave myself"- Rapper T.I.*

"Hey Jarod, this is Mrs. Freeman; give me a call when you get a chance—it's about Manon." This was the day my life changed. This was the day DEPRESSION *knocked on my door.*

Like any other morning, my day started with a smile and a nice cup of coffee. I left the house with great anticipation of my day. I had started a new job that was extremely tiring, yet rewarding—because it was a service job. It was a non-emergency transportation company; where we transported patients to their various appointments (medical, dental, etc.). It was a lot of work: long evenings, and sleepless nights, but I was excited. My older sister was the CEO of the company, and like any good big sister—she employed her baby brother. I must admit, it was challenging working for my older sister—not because she was the "boss" or "supervisor," but because it was a new business, and she was learning it on the go.

That particular morning, when I received the phone call from Mrs. Freeman, my day was already in some sort of a spiral. Despite having my morning joe and smiling cheek-to-cheek, it felt as if the universe had it out for me on this day. About 6:30 that morning, one our emergency vehicles had broken down, an employee had yet to pick up his passenger, and it was close to 100 degrees outside. As one would imagine, it was a pretty rough start.

It was around 8:15am when things settled. I was sitting at my desk, and I heard a noise: "*chirp-chirp.*"

When I looked down at my phone, it was a chirp from my ex-girlfriend. She said, "I heard Manon was shot last night, and I was calling to check on you."

In denial of her statement, I said, "Are you sure?" I would have a received a call by now, I thought to myself.

Nevertheless, I asked her, "Is he ok?"

She responded, "They are saying he died."

I instantly ran outside with premature tears in my eyes, and I shared with her that I would call her back. When I hung up the phone, I noticed that I had seven or eight voicemails. So, I pressed on the first one, and I heard:

"Hey Jarod, this is Mrs. Freeman; give me a call when you get a chance—it's about Manon."

After listening to the next two voicemails (both asking about Manon), I decided to call Mrs. Freeman back. I will never forget her voice. It was a voice that was shattered by what she knew, and had to tell me.

I said, "Mrs. Freeman, please tell me that what I'm hearing about Manon isn't true."

She responded, "Yes, Jarod; it's true."

I fainted.

I literally *passed out*. All I remember is my sister and a neighboring business owner picking me up from the blistering hot pavement. I couldn't believe it.

I was hurt. I was broken. I wanted answers. But mostly, I just wanted my friend back.

God and Me

Have you ever wondered if God cared about humanity? I've always questioned where God was when tragedy struck. In William Young's book *The Shack*, he shares a sense of God in the following passage:

"The problem is that many folks try to grasp some sense of who I am by taking the best version of themselves, projecting that to the nth degree,

*factoring in all the goodness they can perceive,
which often isn't much, and then call that God. And while it
may seem like a noble effort, the truth is that it
falls pitifully short of who I really am. I'm not merely the best
version of you that you can think of. I am far
more than that, above and beyond all that you can ask or
think."*

If God is far above and beyond all that I can ask or think, why even bother in believing in this God? I want a God that's tangible, reachable, and caring. Where was God when my best friend died? Was God there? Was God watching? Did Manon suffer while clinging to life? Did he have to die in front of his house? Why did his mother and father have to be awaken to gunshots outside of their home only to find their son lying lifeless in the grass?

When they lowered Manon's casket on July 2, 2005— pieces of me went with him. In Timothy Keller's book, *Walking with God Through Pain and Suffering*, he affirms parts of my logic surrounding death. His argument is that those of us who sense the wrongness of death-in any form-are correct.

The rage at the dying of the light is our intuition that we were not meant for mortality, for the loss of love, or for the triumph of darkness. In order to help people, face death and grief, we often tell people that death is a perfectly natural part of life. But that asks them to repress a very right and profound human intuition—that we are not meant to simply go to dust, and that love was meant to last.

Manon's death created a space for broken faith. The idea that faith was the substance of things hoped for, and evidence not seen; yeah, that didn't make much sense anymore. Most of my life, I believed in a *just* God: a God who knew everything, and was present everywhere and a God who created the sun to work the day shift, and the moon the night shift. I believed in a God who scattered wall-to-wall carpet across the earth and called it grass, and a God who tilted the earth on its axis causing it to spin and rotate. I believed in a God who created a system that's constantly moving and always in motion and a system that would never be void of movement.

However, after Manon's repass, I no longer believed in *that* God. I believed that God existed, but I didn't believe God was a *good* God.

I stop moving. I stop believing. I stop living.

I Can't Stop Dreaming About His Death

A 2011 article entitle "10 Ways to Make and Be a Best Friend," published by *Psychology Today*, highlights certain aspects of what makes a friend unique. "The essence of friendship is about care and respect. It has nothing to do with money, attractiveness, or "the cool factor." A true friend is there for you, no matter what, and having such a person in your life is a great gift. Manon and I shared an unbreakable bond. A friendship that warranted seven chirps in an hour, and four to five phone sessions a day—perhaps is the reason I still have dreams about his death.

June 25, 2005… I was playing basketball in Morehouse College's Gymnasium when I received seven Nextel chirps within an hour. Yep, you guessed it: It was Manon. It was typical for us to talk that much. Who knew that those last seven chirps would be our last time communicating directly?

The night of Manon's death, I spoke with his younger brother several times. We talked about meeting up at Cascade Skating Rink which we frequented every Sunday night. Nevertheless, after spending quality time with my grandparents and baby cousin, I opted out of going to the skating rink. I called Manon's youngest brother and told him I would catch them tomorrow; but that never happened. Manon was killed a few hours later.

So, what are those dreams about, Dacari?

We had a rule in our clique: *whoever had the most space in their vehicle would always be the one to drive.* Therefore, Manon's Expedition was the preferred vehicle the nights we went out on the town. Typically, we would all meet at Manon's house, park our cars, and prepare to take over the world. The night of Manon's death. those were my exact plans before canceling. Why is this interesting?

Well, when Manon arrived back home from the skating rink that night, a group of guys were waiting for him--with intentions on robbing him for his vehicle. According to court documents and testimonials, the guys proceeded to rob Manon and as a result, he ran. While he was running in fear of his life, a bullet struck the back of head... literally separating his eye from its socket. While taking his last breath, the perpetrators approached his body, took his car keys and drove away. Manon died shortly afterwards.

For years, I had dreams about that night that--if I had been with Manon, if we both would have been dead or if we would have survived it. I would replay the scenario heard in the courtroom about that night and have several, *I wonder if* moments. What if I was there? What if I could have talked them out of it? *What if?* Ultimately, I wondered if I could have saved him. *I Still Haven't Forgiven Myself.*

A year prior to Manon's death, he and I were robbed and held for about 20-25 minutes. It was one of the scariest moments of my life. I didn't know how we would make it out alive. One of the most important moments happened when we were being held.
Manon yelled out to the guys who were robbing us, "Hey I will get you whatever you want; just don't kill my friend!"

Guys, the hardest part about Manon's death is that I was not there the night he died to return that same favor: "Hey I will get you whatever you want; *just don't kill my friend.*"

And I still haven't forgiven myself.

What was I experiencing?

What was happening in my world?
Why couldn't I sleep?
One guess: PTSD.

Psychology Today's article entitled "Post-Traumatic Stress Disorder" reveals that,

PTSD is a psychological disorder that may develop after a traumatic experience, and it is characterized by one symptom that is particularly unique, called "re-experiencing", or more commonly, 'flashbacks.' This is when the memory of a trauma is involuntarily recalled, usually triggered by cues in the environment that are somehow associated to the trauma.

These intrusive trauma memories can be remarkably vivid, overwhelmingly emotional, and are experienced as if they were really happening right then and there." Re-experiencing also occurs in the form of posttraumatic nightmares, considered a "hallmark" of the disorder. Posttraumatic nightmares are generally defined as threatening or frightening dreams that awaken a dreamer and may be marked by any intense negative emotion, such as fear, anger, or even sadness. These nightmares cause significant distress (both during the dream, and after awakening) and may occur several times a week.

So, in 2008, I decided that it was time for me to seek help. I was having recurring nightmares about Manon's death. I was waking up sweaty and crying. I was re-living his murder, and I wasn't there. I saw his body, I saw the clothes, the blood, and the wound. Everything was happening in real-time. I was mentally stuck, and I didn't know what to do. Therefore, with the help of one of my graduate school professors, I visited a

Psychologist at Vanderbilt University's Medical Center. At the completion of my visit I was diagnosed with PTSD.

In general, posttraumatic nightmares are more intense than regular dreams and are similar to waking flashback memories; they contain replays of the actual traumatic event and more scenes of death and violence than normal dreams. At least 50% of PTSD patients suffer from re-experiencing nightmares that incorporate clear elements or even contain exact replications of a traumatic event (termed "replicative nightmares").

Another 20-25% of PTSD patients experience posttraumatic nightmares that are not an exact replay of a trauma memory, but are still often symbolically or indirectly related to the traumatic event. One study examined patients 40 years after a traumatic event and found that patients with replicative nightmares had worse symptoms than patients with non-replicative nightmares. Another study found that trauma survivors who develop PTSD have more replicative nightmares than trauma survivors who do not develop PTSD. Thus, it seems that replicative nightmares are correlated with the development and severity of PTSD "Nightmares after Trauma," *Psychology Today.*

After my diagnosis, I was uncertain of the next steps. Should I seek further counseling? Should I take medicine? I didn't know what to do. I must admit, I was so afraid to share that I had been diagnosed with *anything.* For some odd reason, especially in the black community, if we suffer with something, we are viewed as "weird" or "crazy."

The one thing I didn't want to hear was, "You know Sandra's boy has gone crazy." I didn't want my mom to experience what I saw as an embarrassment. Nevertheless, I took the quiet route, and allowed them to prescribe me medicine.

Yes. I allowed them, because I did not want it.

According to mental health studies, researchers believe that the symptoms of mental illness come from chemical imbalances in a person's brain. "A medication works on these imbalances to reduce your symptoms, or sometimes, to relieve them completely."

But here's the catch: *I stopped taking the medicine.* The medicine would make me sort of *zone out.* I felt empty, more tired, and much more depressed with it, than without it.

As a first-time user of this style of medication, I was unaware of the consistency it took for the medicine to work. And rather than communicating with my physician and getting the medication changed, I stopped taking it, because I felt it didn't work.

What I would later discover about taking medicine for mental illness consist of the following four things noted by Mental Health America:

1. Medications are not cures. Medications only treat symptoms, so if you stop taking them, your symptoms can return.
2. Every medicine has its benefits and its risks. Deciding to take medication is all about balancing possible benefits against possible side effects. Sometimes, it's hard to know how a medicine will affect you until you try it.
3. Medications often help the most when they're part of an overall treatment program. Your plan may include psychotherapy, peer programs and rehabilitative services to help with problems that medication alone can't treat.
4. It can take time to feel better. Some medications take a few weeks to work. And sometimes a medication's side effects may start before its benefits. You also may have to try more than one medication before you get the right fit, but many people find it's worth the wait.

Drugs are the most common treatment for depression in the United States, and there is a widespread belief, popularized by the media, that drugs are the most effective treatment. However, this opinion is not consistent with the results of many carefully conducted outcome studies during the past twenty years. These studies show that the newer forms of psychotherapy, especially cognitive therapy, can be at least as effective as drugs, and for many patients appear to be more effective –"The New Mood Therapy."

This is good news for individuals like me who prefer to be treated without medications due to personal preferences or health concerns. It is also good news for the millions of individuals who have not responded adequately to antidepressants after years and years of treatment and who will still struggle with depression and anxiety. And for more than 10 years, I have committed myself to cognitive therapy. I am firm believer in wrestling with my emotions in order to reach a desirable result that makes me happy.

I went back to medication once, but I eventually let that idea go altogether. Every day is a different journey. I still struggle with understanding why Manon had to die, and the method by which he died. I often think about where my life would be if he was still here, and what we would be doing. I really miss him.

I still haven't forgiven myself.

People say death gets easier to over time, but I would argue that it doesn't—you just learn to adapt without those loved ones. This was my first attack with depression coupled with PTSD. I thought constant therapy and counseling would keep me from relapsing, but it didn't. As you will learn in the following chapters, I hit a major low, but by the Grace of God, I'm still here to write about it.

Are you living with PTSD, and don't know?
Please read information below from
MakeTheConnection.net :

Some of the most common symptoms of PTSD include:

- Recurring nightmare of the traumatic event
- Sleeplessness
- Loss of interest
- Anger or irritability
- Feeling emotionally cut off from others
- Being always on guard
- Having trouble concentrating
- Being easily startled

- These symptoms may not surface for months or years after the actual event occurred, and they may come and go. However, if they persist over time, and disrupt your daily life, then you may have PTSD

Disruptions include:

- Avoiding places or things that remind you of what happened
- Turning to alcohol or drugs to cope with the trauma
- Thoughts of self-harm or harming others
- A need to keep busy with work or other hobbies to occupy your mind
- Isolating yourself

Here's the issue: People who suffer from PTSD may not be able (or willing) to recognize these symptoms and behaviors on their own. They may be aware of them, but are in denial. That's why it's incredibly important for families, friends, and other support circles to be on the lookout for any sign of PTSD early on – the earlier PTSD is addressed, the more successful treatment can be.

Treatment for PTSD

Research has come a long way in recent years, aiding in the effectiveness of PTSD treatment. There are two types of treatment that have been proven effective:

- Counseling
- Medication

Therapy or counseling can help PTSD sufferers understand the reasons behind their thoughts and reactions, and can provide coping strategies to address these challenging situations. Medications can also be used to reduce tension or irritability, as well as to improve sleep. Of course, doctors must provide more detail regarding the best types of medications for each individual case.

Part Two:

Nothing Was the Same

"Somewhere between psychotic and iconic
Somewhere between I want it and I got it
Somewhere between I'm sober and I'm lifted"

"Everyone just wait now
So much on my plate now
People I believed in they don't even show they face now
What they got to say now?
Nothin' they can say now
Nothin' really changed but still they look at me a way now
What more can I say now?
What more can I say now?
You might feel like nothin' was the same"

-Drake

Over the course of grade school, I developed a reputation as the class clown. Honestly, I had no desire other than to make myself and others laugh or smile. Even today, I feel the same way. Seeing others happy is the greatest desire I have. Ergo, the reason I was disruptive in school. Academically, I wasn't the best student. I had the idea that if I just passed the class, that was enough. Who really came to school to work for real? We're here to socialize and have fun, and if learning happens, so be it. Well, that didn't turn out so well. I stayed at in-school suspension, at home suspension, summer school, Saturday school and eventually, I was expelled from high school.

No worries: I enrolled back in school, graduated college twice, and I have a job! My point is not to dwell on the bad, but to ask this one question: *Why did I enjoy being a class clown?* We all have dreams, right? We all grow up desiring to be *something*. We all have a wish to transcend our lives into something beyond the norm--something worth celebrating later in life.

My dream was to become a great actor. I wanted to model my career after Will Smith. I wanted my own comedy television show, and eventually morph into doing dramatic movies. So, going to school and clowning was not just something to do. I wanted to know if I could grab the attention of my classmates and teachers. I believed if I could make them pause and focus their energy and attention on me, I knew I had a strong chance of achieving my goal.

Today, I work full-time in ministry. This is vastly different from where I wanted to be and surprising to so many. So, *how did this happen?*

I've always felt this desire to work for God. As a kid, I would imitate the Pastor, and my sister would be my assistant or nurse. My mother, grandparents, and relatives would always say, "That boy has a call on his life." I would later find out that this meant, for me, God was calling me to ministry or even to pastor. For years, I ran from this idea. I was a class clown and comedian. No one would believe that God would use me to inspire people and bring them to Christ. Oh, but I was so wrong! The more I participated in ministry, the more I saw people who looked like me connect with Christ. So, in spite of my comedic adventures, I found myself in this ministerial space and sought to make a difference.

Millennials and Careers

I'm nervous, yet excited.
I'm about to share an idea with a pastor.
I can't wait to hear his response.
This is almost genius, at least I think so.

Nevertheless, my teenage/young adult self-approached the office of the pastor, "Hey, Pastor; I have an idea. I want to be an actor and a pastor!" The pastor looked confused, but then he stated, "Son, that's mighty ambitious, but you can't do both. You have to pick one." This was one of the first lessons I learned as a millennial: *we're different.* We're not like previous generations. We refuse to live and operate out of one space. And many, like me, gravitate towards the former idea of picking one passion or job and sticking with it. Thus, I decided to pursue ministry full-time, and that's where I am today... *only for TODAY.*

Before we get further into this topic, let's define the term Millennial. There are several definitions, and there is likewise interesting data identifying who and what a millennial is. For this conversation, I will use what the latest data from 2018. According to the Pew Research Center,

The Washington D.C-based think tank, citing more than a decade of research, *declared those born between 1981 and 1996 — or those between the ages of 22 and 37 in 2018 as a part of the millennial generation.*

What does this mean?

The Pew Research Center used some key events to define the millennial generation. It ranged from the terrorist attacks on September 11, 2001, to the historic election of Barack Obama as president in 2008. Of course, there's also the millennial generation's familiarity and ease with technology.

The Pew Research Center's President Michael Dimock wrote:

most millennials came of age and entered the workforce facing the height of an economic recession. The long-term effect of this 'slow start' for millennials will be a factor in American society for decades.

Let's pause here and think for a second. We're dealing with a generation that's politically aware, technological savvy, and culturally sensitive. We've experienced a lot in our short lives—hence sparking the debate on why our level of expertise has spun into multiple passions. When I left the pastor's office that day, I was broken. I didn't think I could achieve my dreams.

I've been walking around for years internally wrestling with working in ministry, and wanting to work with the entertainment industry (radio, tv, film, etc). This is where my heart is. This is where I want to be, *but I'm stuck…* because I was made to believe I had to do one thing.

Was this pastor right? Is it true? Do we have to pick one career or passion and stick with it? Caroline Beaton wrote an article on Forbes.com declaring that "Millennials--choosing one door to walk through means all the other doors close, and there's no ability to return back to that path." So rather than go through any doorway, it's better to stand in the atrium and gaze.

The truth is, I would rather stand in the corridor of opportunities than select one thing that could expire.

Here's what may surprise those generations before us: We love to work. We're not a lazy or entitled generation. Remember: we're the generation that followed the rules. Our parents (baby boomers) told us, "go to school, get a good education, and you will find a good job."

Ha! Yeah, we tried that.

It didn't work. We were forced to believe that our degrees didn't mean a thing. Many of us went back to school to get a second degree and others settled for jobs in order to save the embarrassment of not having one. In a real sense, we were bamboozled by a system. Chris Hayes, author of "Twilight of Elites: America After Meritocracy," states,

We do not trust our institutions, because they have shown themselves to be untrustworthy. The drumbeat of institutional failure echoes among the populace as skepticism. And given the scope and depth of this distrust, it's clear that we are in the midst of a broad and devastating crisis of authority.

The reality is this: We do not trust institutions as previous generations have. Therefore, this explains how we work, and why our demands are similar yet different.

According to <u>Time Magazine</u>, polls show that "millennials want flexible work schedules, more 'me time' on the job, and nearly nonstop feedback and career advice from managers." Moreover, and most important to the millennial generation is that we only switch jobs when it makes sense, and opportunities are limited. Like any other generation, when it comes to careers, steady work with compensation and good benefits, along with an opportunity to learn and grow, is the common thread.

Guys, dealing with social institutions regarding becoming/being a professional became *depressing.*

Millennials and Faith

Sitting in a crowded Atlanta airport-music blasting through my earphones, I was approached by my pastor. He stated, "You must be listening to Jay Z?" I replied, "No, I am actually listening to T.I. this morning." He paused, smiled, and said, "What am I going to do with this generation? You all know hip-hop, but you don't know a hymn."

After his statement, I immediately felt convicted—convicted in the sense that it was true—I do know more hip-hop lyrics than I do church hymns.

A few weeks later I begin to examine the "why" of this. Why is it that I know more hip-hop lyrics than I do hymns? I began to question the validity of my Christian walk. Am I less saved, hypocritical, or a secular being pretending to be Christian? However, as I was doing spiritual acrobatics in my mind, I discovered two things: 1-I was never taught hymns, and in addition to this, 2-I found that many of the hip-hop songs that I listened to, spoke to my experience, and personal walk with God. In essence, I relate more to hip-hop lyrics than I do hymns.

Why is this? I grew up in an environment where the hustler was more visible than the prophet. The hustler was the common man; he was the approachable one. The prophet was the one who was revered. We were afraid to speak to the pastor, the prophet, because we were taught to fear God, and these men were the closest vessels to God, so we never embraced interaction. Therefore, my encounter with the hustler was normal, and I embraced every moment of the interactions. I embraced the hustler because of the messages he/she projected were those of the hip-hop movement.

See, the hip-hop movement spoke on facts, what people saw, and how to exist in that environment. The pastor/prophet spoke on what they knew based on their faith. So, for me, it was a clash between facts and faith. Therefore, as a kid, facts were more important than faith, so I adapted to two of my senses: what I could *see* and *hear*. As I grew in my faith, I became curious as to how to integrate both worlds.

After studying faith, religion, and completing divinity school, I realized that hymns and hip-hop were similar in this regard. They both spoke to individual experiences that lead them to a belief. Hymns point to God and a life to live as Christ, and hip-hop points to how one can engage in a cruel society where oppression, subjection, and depression thrive.

We are now engaged in two worlds: one is a text that directs you to live as Christ, and the other that causes you to examine what Christ disliked.

Hip-hop culture became a way of dealing with the hardships of life, as minorities within America, and an outlet to deal with violence and gang culture. Hip hop gave young African Americans a voice to let their issues be heard. As Manthia Diawara writes in *In Search of Africa*, "Like rock-and-roll, hip-hop is vigorously opposed by conservatives because it romanticizes violence, law-breaking, and gangs. It also gave young blacks a chance for financial gain by "reducing the rest of the world to consumers of its social concerns."

Therefore, the issue is not so much hip-hop over or against hymns as it is the expression of belief. Though many of the hip-hop lyrics won't directly point me to Jesus, with my faith, as I listen, it gives me greater clarity on how I should live like Jesus. For Jesus declared his mission in Luke 4:18: *"The Spirit of the Lord is on me, because he has anointed me to proclaim good news to the poor. He has sent me to proclaim freedom for the prisoners and recovery of sight for the blind, to set the oppressed free" (NIV).*

Thus, I must live out his mission by bringing healing and wholeness to a broken people and a broken society.

Now my issue with hymns is that no one taught me them. I assume that as kids, we're supposed to catch on, and eventually these lyrics will be embedded into our souls like our foundational Christian beliefs. Yet, they were not, so I turned to what I could understand. Maybe we lost the fabric of our tradition in the African-American church: *an oral tradition*. Maybe we forgot to pass down traditions that sustain a people during hard times?

The World affairs council of Houston put it like this,

African-American culture has always passed down important information to the next generation. African-based oral traditions became the primary means of preserving history, mores, and other cultural information among the people. This was consistent with the *griot* practices of oral history in many African and other cultures that did not rely on the written word. Many of these cultural elements have been passed from generation to generation through storytelling.

Yet, I never learned hymns as I did scripture. We always had bible quiz bowls but never hymn quizzes. Therefore, how would I know unless I had a strong desire to learn them for myself?

Nevertheless, there is no one to blame unless, somehow, someway, I know more hip-hop than hymns misrepresent the Church and the Christian faith. If this is the case, and I am misrepresenting my faith, so let us examine the origin of a hymn to hip-hop lyrics.

Hymns are essentially a genre of song that have been written to offer honor, praise or prayer to a particular deity. Taken from the Greek term *hymnos*, it is literally a song of praise. If these are songs of adoration, and praise to God, does

one lose their Christian rights if I embraced T.I.'s lyrics in his
song "Praying for Help," when he recites:

"I know it's only one king, one thing, one being only something
I believe without seeing
And with all my faith
I pray somehow, some way, regardless of what anyone say
I believe one day
That Ima change my life, get right, start living like Christ, to the
end of my fight?"

So, is there something wrong if I identify with his lyrics more
so than these: *"He's the Lily of the Valley, the Bright and*
Morning Star, He's the fairest of ten thousand to my soul?"

Contextually, what if I have no idea what a lily is, and
my valley is an alley where homelessness and poverty exist…a
place where I made money selling narcotics? One could then
see how I could identify with the former lyrics more than the
latter.

One of the challenges with hymns is that we are
relegated to singing songs with no context of the individuals
who wrote them or the experiences that lead them to write the
hymn. The life of a hip-hop artist is always on
display…negatively or positively. Thus, we as consumers or
fans watch these artists evolve or dissolve. *The church is*
hidden. We won't share our stories or experiences that have
lead us to Christ or stories that help to empower and inspire
people.

My argument therefore is this: if the church's desire is
to have productive dialogue and great worship practices with
this new generation, she has to become transparent and more
vulnerable in expressing God. I agree with F. Douglas Powe Jr,
when he says:

The evangelistic crisis they (churches) face is their inability to embody the good news of Jesus Christ in a way that speaks to those in the post-civil rights generations. Hip-hop does not have a problem saying I sinned, as a matter of fact, their sin is on display. The church must admit that we are imperfect, and are constantly working out or salvation with trembling and fear.

What does all of this say about Millennials and Faith? According to Michael Hout, Professor of sociology at New York University, "many millennials have parents who are baby boomers, and boomers expressed to their children that it's important to think for themselves – that they find their own moral compass." My previous argument about Hip-Hop & Hymns was as such: my mother introduced me to Christ at a young age, but she allowed me to wrestle with the ideas of Christianity. Her position was one that encouraged me to think and do for myself; hence, why many think Millennials are *flighty* and *weird*.

We're none of those things.
We are not bound to systems and institutions.
We love God, but we wrestle with God's Church.

To further understand this, think of it this way: Professor Hout continues his argument by bringing up an issue that we mentioned previously: *trust*. He argues, "younger people, particularly, are not as confident as older adults when it comes to institutions like the press, government and churches." On a political note, there have been so many issues during our time that make it hard for us to trust the institutions that are still in place today. Perhaps they were already shaky, well established before my generation's time and even more unreliable to us now.

In his article, Millennials and Religion, Rabbi Wildes states, *"Millennials treasure meaning and purpose in much of what they do, especially in their work and in relationships, along with positive "do-good" mission trips."* This is a fact—if you attach the religious experience to do-good services, and messages that highlight meaning and values, you will gain a greater perspective on how we view faith.

Guys, attempting to bridge the gap for understanding of expressed personal beliefs became *depressing.*

Millennials and Family

According to an article written by Jennifer Calfas,

A large majority of young Americans now believe education and economic accomplishments are extremely important parts of adulthood, and more than half — 55%, believe marrying and having children is not very important. That mentality differs from the values of 40 years ago. In 1975, 8 in 10 people were married by the time they turned 30. Now, 8 in 10 are married by the time they turn 45.

The latest Gallup poll taken suggested that most millennials have not yet married, and they are waiting longer to marry.

For 34-year-olds, just over half (56%) are married, and of these, 83% have children. But a substantial number (46%) of those who have never been married and are well into their 30s have children. This may represent a seismic shift in the connection between marriage and child rearing because as recently as 2000, the comparable percentage of single/never married 30- to 34-year-olds with children was just 30%.

Essentially, it has been presented that because many millennials live in a multi-adult household, that much of what we encounter are domestic partnerships and because of this, we are more likely to identify with communities like the LGBT. In turn, it suggests that this identification make us much more prone to change the social standards of our day.

I've heard it argued that we have no moral standards, and we allow anything to fly and *I don't believe it's true.*

What has changed? What's different? I would argue the theme of *trust.* What many of us know compared to other generations are certain truths that families tried to cover up. We're familiar with granddaddy's "outside kids," Uncle Joe" molesting cousin "Nina," and a host of other things. Yes, we applaud the couple who has been married for 40 years, but we know the truth that for 33 of those years, they slept in different rooms. We're more knowledgeable of these things which is why we are more cautious to dive into marriage as quickly as previous generations.

When you think of having and raising kids, millennials are more cautious about this area too. I remember when I got married in 2011; the next question after the reception was, "when are you guys having kids?" Well in 2015, we had our first child, and the next questions was, "when are you guys having another one? You know, it's good to have them back-to-back." What many failed to realize is that our idea of family is also tied to our socioeconomic status.

According to Andrea Flynn's article, "Shifting Work and Families: Trends Among Millennials," she writes,

The Great Recession affected U.S. workers of all ages, but it had a disproportionate impact on the millennial generation. Unemployment rates among this cohort remain high at 15.2 percent for those ages 18 to 29, while underemployment rates are even higher at 40 percent.1 The ranks of unemployed Millennials now total 4.6 million, nearly 40 percent of all U.S. unemployed workers.

The fact is *we're BROKE!* Childcare costs, and affordable housing are key factors in our decision to create the "American family" that we previously knew.

To end this chapter, I take a thought from Simon Sinek's interview, "Millennials in the Workplace." In an abbreviated form, below are a few points he makes about millennials in the in general:

1. *The generation that is called the millennials, too many of them grew up subject to "failed parenting strategies." Where they were told that they were special - all the time, they were told they can have anything they want in life, just because they want it.*

2. *You take this group of people and they graduate and they get a job and they're thrust into the real world and in an instant, they find out they are not special, their moms can't get them a promotion, that you get nothing for coming in last and by the way you can't just have it because you want it. In an instant, their entire self-image is shattered. So, we have an entire generation that is growing up with lower self-esteem than previous generations.*

3. *The other problem to compound it is we are growing up in a Facebook/Instagram world, in other words, we are good at putting filters on things. We're good at showing people that life is amazing even though I am depressed...*

4. *So, you have an entire generation growing up with lower self-esteem than previous generations - through no fault of their own, they were dealt a bad hand. Now let's add in technology...it's highly, highly addictive...We have age restrictions on smoking, drinking and gambling but we have no age restrictions on social media and cell phones. Which is the equivalent of opening up the liquor cabinet and saying to our teenagers "hey by the way, if this adolescence thing gets you down - help yourself."*

5. *Why is this important? Almost every alcoholic discovered alcohol when they were teenagers. Social stress, financial stress, career stress, that's pretty much the primary reasons why an alcoholic drinks. But now because we are allowing unfettered access to these devices and media, basically it is becoming hard wired and what we are seeing is that they grow older, too many kids don't know how to form deep, meaningful relationships. "Their words, not mine."*

6. *They will admit that many of their relationships are superficial...so, when significant stress begins to show up in their lives, they're not turning to a person, they're turning to a device, they're turning to social media, they're turning to these things which offer temporary relief.*

In essence, I thought this to be important for the reader, because without proper context of who the millennial is, it will be difficult to understand the following chapters as I elaborate on depression and how it affected me from a faith, business, and family perspective. As we go deeper in the following chapters, remember: *we're on this journey together.*

Guys, trying to establish a family based on what society suggested I do became *depressing.*

Part Three:

I Let Bishop Down

Long live the idols, may they never be your rivals
Pastors were like Jesus, The Elders wrote the Bible
Now what you're 'bout to hear's a tale of glory and sin
Bishop Joseph W. Walker, III my mentor, that's how the story
end

-A play on J.Cole's Words remixed by Dacari J. Middlebrooks

November 7, 2010, I was afforded the opportunity to speak at our nightly worship service. At the close of the service, my then Fiancé and I were invited over to my Pastor's home. I was slightly nervous and, honestly, I was thinking, "What did I do wrong?" People shared that they enjoyed my message; even one our prominent mothers of the church stated, "Baby, you've got it." Surely, I didn't disappoint anyone...or maybe *I'd Let Bishop Down.*

Once there, my anxiety was intensified as I was offered the role to become my pastor's assistant. I didn't know what it meant! Was this something that could truly help me in ministry? Would this be the beginning of something great? I would soon find out, because a month after the initial offer, I said "yes" to the position.

So, here we go...

It was late in the evening, and the sun was going down. I was drained from the day, and extremely tired. I worked alongside my pastor by assisting him with four of our weekly services, but our work was not done. Pastor and I arrived had to make a hospital visit. One of our members, and her family, were in the process of removing one of their family members off life support. This was a tough one for me, I didn't want to be present for this. I rejected the idea of staying in the room to witness that moment. I asked, "Bishop/Pastor, do you mind if I wait outside of the door? This is difficult to watch." He replied with, "No problem; I understand."

Who knew, however, that my position as first assistant to the bishop/my pastor would require me to stay on the outside of doors figuratively and literally, because it became *difficult to watch.*

Over the course of three and half years, it became *difficult to watch.* I witnessed pastors debate over doctrine, church members fight over pews, ecclesiastical scholars critique the church without ever attending, and armor bearers learn the art of armor bearing. All of these things were important in my formation, but one thing in particular became a thorn in my flesh: it was this idea of what an armor bearer was, and was supposed to do. It led me to process faith and ministry differently.

I've always struggled with the idea of what an Armor bearer was and its functions. Most armor bearers are defined in scripture through passages such as Judges 9:54,1 Samuel 16:21, 1 Samuel 14:6-17, 2 Samuel 18:15. For millennials who are involved in church, we know this to be a bit more figurative that previously considered. And to be honest, I never knew how being an armor-bearer really aided the pastor. Many of my colleagues who functioned as armor-bearers loved it, but I saw it as an enabling the pastor. I was responsible for carrying my pastor's bible and manuscript into the pulpit, doing personal chores for he and his family all the while being his eyes and ears for ministerial engagement. Let me be clear: I did not have a problem with the roles and function; I had a problem with the job because it was not what I was told I would be doing.

When the position was offered, I was told that I would be traveling a lot and seeing the world... which I did. But I also thought I would have a chance to teach, and really engage in ministerial activities. However, in the course of three and half years as his assistant, I only taught twice, and rarely spent time helping with ministry development and ministry structure. I saw my dreams unrealized. I wanted more. I didn't want to be on the outside of ministry watching. I wanted to be deeply involved in the life of the church. I wanted to create new ministries that impacted multiple generations. I wanted to teach often. I believed in my oratory skills, and my ability to get our congregants to think, and act. I knew I was gifted, but I was restricted. I knew I was anointed to do more, but being a personal assistant kept me anonymous, and relegated me to underwhelming tasks.

In a sense, I felt bamboozled, and I was angry. Like that day at the hospital, I was looking through a glass of disappointment, and it became *difficult to watch*.

What pastors and leaders must understand is that there is a new paradigm shift in understanding this whole idea of serving (being an armor-bearer). One of the challenges with serving leaders in the church is that many of them have preconceived notions of how they should be served. There is no collaborative conversation about what serving is or what it means to the person who will be serving. The depiction of how one is treated in regard to serving has been relegated to a model of slavery. Many of these leaders do not see how they use and take advantage of those who serve them. It is disrespectful for a leader to enter the boardroom of consciousness, yet think only about themselves, and their personal needs. If Jesus believed that he was sent to the earth to serve, and not be served, why do our ministerial leaders feel they should? You can't preach Jesus, teach Jesus, and not practice Jesus. It doesn't make sense.

We desire to create a new model that resembles the life of Jesus and not that of personality driven leadership. It's not about the man or woman; it's the message of Jesus: who He is, and what He did that we're after. Though we stand alongside of our leaders as they minister to God's people, we desire to participate in the deliverance of the people. We want to be involved. We don't want to be on the outside looking in. Create a space for us, and allow us to manage and win in that space.

Guys, having us in worship, but not making room for us to serve is *depressing*.

I Didn't Sign Up for This

I graduated from Morehouse College in 2006 with a Bachelor of Arts in Mass Communications with a concentration in Radio/Television/Film. In 2010, I earned a Master of Divinity degree from Vanderbilt University in Nashville, TN.

When I was offered the position to be my pastor's assistant, I expected upward mobility and growth within the organization, flexibility, but more importantly: decent pay. This isn't what I signed up for. I felt slighted.

My pastor has a saying about Millennials. He says, "You guys are so flighty, and you all aren't loyal to anything." I often smile, and share that he's *partially* right.

We do hop from job-to-job, church-to-church, etc. However, we go to places where establishing meaning is vital and vision is progressive. Thus, if you judge us without context, your assumption may be valid. Yet, if you look through our lens, you may find a truth that what you're offering is stale, unimpressive, and lacks meaning. We want more and at the heart of this: I wanted more. I wanted more opportunity and more pay.

I agree with David Carlson's article *"It's Simple, Millennials Want More Money"* where he says, "what people argue is that millennials care more about their work environment, work-life balance, and engagement with their job than they do about their compensation. While I'm not denying that millennials care about lifestyle factors like these, I think that the studies support a very simple fact: at the end of the day millennials want more money."

It's true! We love relaxing working environments, causal clothing, air pods, iPad, etc. But we want to be PAID. We want fair compensation for the work we're doing.

It's been noted and proven that the disparity in economic means is an issue for millennials. And while many millennials have a source of income, they spent much of their time at work worrying about their financial responsibilities. If you put yourself in the shoes of someone who has student loans and various financial obligations, combine that with the fact that they are making entry-level pay, is it any surprise that a focus of millennials is their compensation?

My Pastor and older employees of our organization laugh when we talk about pay…considering what they were paid when they were my age. One shared, "I made 30k a year, and lived in an apartment." Yeah, 30k in the 1980's wasn't bad. I think gen x'ers and baby boomers forget that the price of living was lower. When I was in high school gas was $0.69 cents a gallon. I used to fill up my tank for six to seven dollars! The reality is, it's not equal. We do not share the same journey, and frankly, it's not fair. Yet they wonder why we job hop.

Let's examine research from Carlson, and others,

A recent Staples Business Advantage Survey found that 52% of millennials who changed jobs in the last 12 months have done so for a salary increase. Additionally, 68% of millennials believed an increase in pay would improve workplace happiness. Based on all the evidence that millennials are stressed out over finances, it's not surprising that having a higher income is a priority for them and is something they think will improve overall happiness.

I love Carlson's final statement regarding this issue:

The millennial's focus on increasing their income isn't about ENTITLEMENT. It's about being strategic and making sure they are able to make as much money as they possibly can and, in turn, having more options and opportunities.

I didn't sign up to do the job of ten people only be paid one salary. Being a first assistant was difficult. I was not paid a fair wage, and this constantly tormented my soul. I felt inadequate, and devalued. I was overworked, and underpaid. I became sad, disappointed, and started wearing my feelings on my sleeve.

Guys, wearing my heart on my sleeve became *depressing.*

I Hate My Job

I conducted an Instagram poll a few weeks ago, asking my audience if they hated their jobs. Of my 4k followers, over 80% are perceived Millennials. About 100 of them participated in the poll. I received some surprising results. Only 24% of them polled that they hated their jobs, while 76% of them stated "No." Those who shared "No," noted that they didn't hate their jobs, they just didn't care for the positions they held at their jobs. Many of them were searching for meaning, and their jobs hadn't offered that.

In 2014, Karl Moore, a contributing writer for Forbes shared some of our sentiments. He talked about how employers have to create an environment where young employees have to find purpose which will enable them to envision a future with your company.

Young people are not static. They are on an endless search for happiness. If an organization is unable to map out a road plan or a purpose of employment, it will unfortunately notice a high 0-2-year turnover rate and have struggle with employee retention. Millennials need direction and meaning...an interesting mixture of altruism and self-interest. As far as millennials are concerned, they want their employers to embrace change and adapt to their needs. And they should. After all, we are the future of all companies.

I was searching for meaning, and I couldn't find it in the work I was doing. I was very busy, yet I was empty. I realize now that you will never be as happy as you would like until you recognize why you're here. I believe there's nothing more detrimental to one's existence than *being faithful to the wrong assignment*. Hear me: **I didn't hate my job or my pastor—I just didn't like what I was doing.**

So, my bishop took a chance on me.

That night after I left Bishop's house, the night he offered me the job, was the night he took a chance on me. He took a kid who is a hip hop enthusiast, student of culture and trend, and created a space for me to work with him in ministry!

Many of my colleagues would have *died*, not literally though, to work with Bishop. He is well known around the world. He took a church from 175 members, and it has grown to over 30k members. Thus, for me to be his assistant was huge! This was the dream ticket. This was the moment young preachers/ministers, etc. dream of. So Dacari: I'm not understanding why was there room for depression?

We had seven weekly services, traveled to other cities in between, weddings and funerals on Saturday's—It was a lot. I was a newlywed, had a new home, and was barely there to enjoy both. Now, my wife and I both knew the sacrifice we would have to make, which we were fine with, but it was draining. Honestly, I had no life, no "me time." All of my free time was spent trying to be a husband, son, brother, and friend. I was crumbling, and I needed a shift, and Bishop granted it.

After a three-and-a-half-year period as an assistant, Bishop granted me another opportunity. He appointed me to oversee about 80% of ministerial activities. I was excited—it was finally time for growth, and a raise. Everything was going well the first month, but then I hit a road block. I was confronted with a truth that I avoided most of my life.

Guys, how could the opportunity of a lifetime be coupled with the feeling of depression?

Dacari Is a Threat

I am a creative. I love innovation, art, and imagination. I'm very optimistic. I believe anything can work. I believe in a hopeful future, and I am always excited about the present. So, what happened?

When I transitioned into my new role, my managerial reporting structure changed. This was no surprise to me, and I was actually excited about my new manager. We had gotten along so well in the three years prior, so I didn't see it as a problem. However, I must note that over the course of three years, I'd heard complaints from other employees about our manager's style of leadership. This manager operated from a top-down power structure. Whatever this manager said, that's what it was. And yes, I learned this pretty quickly.

About a week into the new role, I was late turning in a report. When I apologized about it, the vocal response was weird: "Hey man, no problem, but don't let it happen again." Now, I understand that when work is due—it's due, but I was a week into the new role, and didn't know what I was doing. Besides, I considered us as pretty good acquaintances, so no need for the "dad response." Yet, that was not the first time nor was it the last time I would encounter this behavior. Most of what I did was critiqued heavily. My work was always in question even if my Pastor loved it. Small things became an issue such as me not wearing a tie on a particular day because we couldn't determine what business causal was (a month-to-month wardrobe rule that we still haven't solved).

There were minute complaints that, to this day, I believe were made up. It became a toxic working environment, and I was not happy. I dreaded waking up and going into the office. The mere presence of my manager agitated my soul. *It's amazing how a person's presence can change your mood, and if you're not careful—your job performance.* Over the course of a year, while under this manager's supervision, there were weekly digital sparring matches, non-verbal actions that showed the dislike amongst the two of us, and just overall harassment. I like how Liz Ryan talks about this issue. She mentions this issue in a Forbes article:

One day, you're chugging along in your job and everything is going well. Your boss is complimentary and supportive of you and your goals. Suddenly, everything shifts. Something is wrong. Now, you can't seem to do anything right. Your manager picks at you over insignificant things. No matter how hard you try, you can't please your boss. What's wrong? You were high on your manager's list of star performers, and now you're one of their least favorite people.

I was so confused. It hit me like a ton of bricks. I was completing all of my assignments. I implemented ideas, and added value to the ministry. Even today, when you receive a first-time visitor's package at our church, that was something I brought to our ministry. If you see first time visitor's parking at our church, that was a vision I gave to our Pastor. If you get a new member's booklet, that was something that I created with a great team of people. It was my idea. If you receive a text message from our ministry, that was something I brought to our team. There are several things you can see where I added valued to our ministry; so why was I receiving so much hate?

I think Liz sums it up well, *"Many fearful bosses cannot handle having a person on their team who might someday outshine them. They will signal their discontent by squashing you like a bug -- or at least trying to."*

Let me take a guess at this? I could be wrong about it all, but I'm certain there's some truth to this. This particular manager was the youngest on the team, prior to my arrival, and possibly the most energetic and creative. This is important to note because my pastor is the same. He has high energy and he's creative, so attracting people with similar skills is important to his ministry. Therefore, I show up with not just creativity, but a new wave of exposure.

I brought something unique to our team. I was not only the youngest on our executive team, but I was second behind our pastor as it relates to education. I had attended prominent institutions, worked and volunteered with organizations well beyond church spaces. My lens was different, so I challenged a lot of things we did. Trust me, this brought some dis-ease to our team. My pastor began to lean on me for ideas...ideas he would have normally gotten from this manager. I could tell that it bothered the manager. The non-verbal clues, head shakes, and the unnecessary rebuttals made it clear that I was a threat.

I'm used to the word "hater." I heard it a lot, but I never fully embraced the idea of it. There are several meanings regarding this word, but the most relative is *a person that simply cannot be **happy** for another person's success. So, rather than be happy, they make a point of exposing a flaw in that person.* Listen, I could be wrong, again, but I will argue this point forever. This manager was a HATER...period. I remember this manager canceled an entire course that I'd planned to teach, because they believed that it was not faith-based disregarding the fact that I was teaching the course to churches around the country.

In addition, that same week, the manager called another employee who was editing a video that I featured in, and told the editor to delete some of the scenes I was in, because I was "seen too much." In that statement alone was the issue: I was a threat to the attention that this manager was used to receiving. I was different; I was nothing like what they had seen before. People embraced me differently. Though I am an ordained elder, I function as I always have: Dacari J. Middlebrooks- a kid from Mechanicsville (Community centrally located in downtown Atlanta). I was liked, and my authenticity to remain myself created the resentment, and hate.

Ok, Dacari...speak more about this and its effects.

Very well.

I didn't know this would affect me so deeply, but it did. My anger turned into a deep sadness. For the first time in my life, I was looking for acceptance. I wanted to be respected and seen as a valuable member of the team, but, I didn't feel the part. I felt neglected, and devalued. I didn't previously know what it was like to feel unwanted. This was a hard space to be in considering I've always been popular even as the consistent class clown. This became one of the moments in my life where I deferred attention. I wanted to dim my light, and allow this person to become whatever they needed to become, so they would stop bothering me.

Quite frankly, I was hurt. And as Deepak Chopra once stated,

It's hard to admit, but wherever a relationship exists, the possibility of someone getting wounded exists. The most common reason we get hurt by another person is: Our ideas of hurt don't match.

I learned to respect boundaries. I learned to feel secure in who I was and make others feel secure. I expected to be respected for my opinions, even if the other person disagrees with them. I understood that each person has emotionally sensitive areas that need to be handled delicately. I recognized that you don't point out other people's faults. You don't automatically find fault or argue just to get a rise out of someone. You listen even if you don't agree with the other person. My *default* position is to *accept rather than to reject*. I am genuinely happy when the other person succeeds.

My boundaries were infringed upon—causing an internal battle within myself. I questioned who I was, and why I was still working for the church. I was hurt. I was angry. I was sad. *I wanted out, so I looked for the exit.*

A Letter to Bishop

Hey Bishop,

It's me again. Just wanted to apologize. You've been one of the most influential guys in my life. You took a chance on me, and gave me every opportunity I asked for. You've been more than what you had to be for me. At times, I felt entitled to certain things—partially my fault, others due to being told I could have these things.

Let me say this, and give you this truth: in 2013, I told my wife to apply for that position at Emory University in Atlanta. I was emotionally drained by the church and Nashville in general. I didn't feel valued. I felt betrayed by a system that told us we would be rewarded if we went to school and get an education. I was angry because of my STARTING PAY. I thought I was slighted. I truly believed like many millennials that our degrees would aid in a promising salary, but it didn't. I was grateful for it but didn't feel it was a fair wage.

Also, I didn't like how the first assistant position was portrayed. I didn't like how Pastor's treated those who served them...definitely not you, but I really didn't like the personal stuff. I recognize the need, but I was just uncomfortable in that space. I wanted to push the ministry forward. I wanted more opportunities to help us win. Sidebar: I've always hated how armor bearers had to sit outside of rooms while the Bishop's ate. I didn't like and still dislike that. Who came up with that crap?

You said to me once, "Dacari, I believe you think there are some things beneath you." I can answer that honestly now, and say "Yes, there are some things that are beneath me." This is not to say that I'm better than anyone or anything, but some things I just didn't sign up for. Bishop, we didn't necessarily have to leave Nashville. I wanted to work with the marketing and media department. But we needed another position filled, so I worked it. I did the best I could in that role, and hopefully, you were pleased. I'm sorry Bishop, but I felt I had to leave. I had to leave because I couldn't work with the supervisor you left in charge. They understood your methods, but in my opinion, they lacked your heart. I had to go; I couldn't stay in that environment. It was toxic, it was draining my creativity, and my overall passion for ministry. You allowed me to leave the city, but kept me employed, and paid me well. I'm so grateful now, but I am also sorry....

Bishop, I'm sorry because you've been the best mentor and friend I could have. You've given me everything I've asked for. You made sure I stayed employed. You made sure I didn't lack in any area of my life. You looked and continue to look after me, but Bishop I QUIT ON YOU, and I'm so sorry. I'm so grateful to have you in my life. I will always have your back, and will always stay down with you, but I am so sorry... because I LET YOU DOWN.

-Dacari

If you're struggling with your current job, answer the following questions, because I want you to win:

- *Are you underpaid?* If you plan to leave, why not show the data and make a strong case for a raise?
- *Is it a lack of work/life balance?* Perhaps your employer would be open to you working from home a few days a week, flexible hours, or a reduction of hours if it was the only way they could keep you.
- *Is it boredom or a lack of challenge?* Switching teams at your existing employer might be incredibly refreshing. Or, maybe your boss would be open to moving you to a new project.
- *Is it overwhelming bureaucracy and soul-sucking drudgery?* In this case, it's probably time to move on.

Part Four:

The Fade to Black

I pray I'm forgiven
For every bad decision I made
Every sister I played
Cause I'm still paranoid to this day
And it's nobody fault I made the decisions I made
This is the life I chose or rather the life that chose me
If you can't respect that your whole perspective is whack
Maybe you'll love me when I fade to black

-Jay Z

My wife and I packed up our home in Nashville and headed back to Atlanta. Atlanta: the place where we met, where we took our engagement pictures, and the place where we tied the knot. Atlanta is my home, my sacred, and safe place. It was the place where I grew up. The place where my wife and I declared would be our last move. The place where we would have our kids, and grow our family. Oh, Atlanta... Hot-Lanta.

When my wife and I moved back to Atlanta, we were both excited. It was a huge relief from the city we had called home for 7-8 years. We were back in the city with my childhood friends, fraternity brothers, her sorority sisters, and new colleagues. This was it. It was a new beginning for us both, and we were ready to begin the next chapter of our lives. However, I ran into a slight problem: I was back in a familiar city, but I was in an unfamiliar space; I couldn't find my friends.

Wait, where were my friends?

Friendships are highly important to me. I value my friends. I believe in our connections, and I try to honor those connections by being present, authentic, and loving. I believe relationships in general gives us a sense of purpose and belonging. I believe we need human interactions to survive this life, so, yes friendships are very important to me.

According to Christopher Griffin, research finds that,

As social creatures, human beings are motivated to be affiliated with others and have a sense of belongingness in meaningful relationships outside that of family, and that a lack of these interpersonal relationships has a significant negative impact on psychological, emotional, and physical health. Better social networks are associated with more favorable health outcomes, better coping with life stressors, and increases in positive subjective experiences. Close and meaningful relationships may even be necessary in order to achieve the experience of high well-being. Thus, friendships can be psychologically adaptive, fostering high well-being and a state of good mental health.

In addition, Jane Collingwood's article on "The Importance of Friendship" argues,
"causes of modern social problems, from divorce to homelessness and obesity, are often thought to be based in areas such as poverty, stress or unhappiness. But researchers suggest we are overlooking something crucial: *friendship*. It would appear that our society is ignoring its importance."

People underestimate friendships. Why are they so significant? How is it relative to my depression and living a full life?

On Jay Z's Album Magna Carta Holy Grail, he has an amazing song about family. The song is called La Familia, and on it he declares these words:

My brothers is my brother like my brother is,
my niggas is my brother like my mother kids.
Not just in good times,
that's that sucka shit,
but in war times,
it's just what it is.

I couldn't find my brothers, and I found great pain in that.

Prior to moving to Atlanta, I contacted many of my friends, living in Atlanta, to share with them that I would be returning to the city. I began to share my desires of what I wanted to accomplish once I returned, and many of them assured me that they would assist. Before I elaborate, remember earlier when I mentioned that my initial desire in life was to become this great actor and live in Hollywood? Thus, returning to Atlanta, I figured I would recover that dream again and attempt to live it out. So, in sharing these dreams, I had an expectation that once I moved, I would gain the connections and resources needed to live this dream.

I must admit, however; that I didn't come back to Atlanta to act, but I wanted to work in the industry. I wanted to connect in all phases of mass communications. I saw from social media that many of my friends were hanging out and working with many of the stakeholders of the industry, so, in my opinion, I was sure to connect when I returned.

After the first few months of being back in Atlanta, I'd yet to connect with anyone in any of the areas I was interested in. I was confused. If my friends had these resources available, why wouldn't they share them? What I would soon discover is that social media creates false illusions and false realities. I learned that cool pictures with celebrities didn't equate to authentic relationships. I realized that my friends knew key industry leaders due to business, but never garnered personal relationships with these figures. They didn't know who we thought they knew. Great people, but they had no power to connect the dots.

In addition to not offering to aid me with the career resources, I was seldom invited to social gatherings. I would see many of these things via social media and on one occasion, even ran into a few of them while randomly trying to create a new social life on my own. What was happening in my world? Everything I once knew was different. I started to feel alone, and because of these emotions, I began to isolate myself which creating more division and ultimately loneliness.

I wanted the connections I had prior to moving to Nashville, but they were no longer there. While this stung, I have to admit that I didn't do a good job either after feeling rejected by my circle of friends. Not once did I mention to those who I thought I was close with that I felt left out and excluded. I was also gone for seven years and many of them had to adapt without me as well. They had to foster new relationships and live their lives.

To this day, I'm unsure how many of my friendships have gone from "that's my homeboy" to "we're cool." Whatever the case, I allowed my feelings to create illusions, and now I'm forced to pick up the pieces and rebuild. I internalized and created false assumptions about our relationships. I would say things like, "they don't care about me, so why bother to care about them?"

I was *sad*. I created my own offenses, and wanted sympathy, and support.

But my hard truth is in Jennifer Smith's article about friendship and depression:

Keeping friends when you have depression can be difficult. Often those of us with depression exert a great deal of energy in simply accomplishing daily tasks, practicing self-care, and caring for our families. It can feel like maintaining friendships is the last thing we have time for; however, keeping friends when you have depression is an important part of learning to cope.

In essence, it's not *where are my friends, it's where is Dacari?*" It's not that I couldn't find my friends, but *they couldn't find me*. I'd left the circle.

Oh No, Baby!
What Is You Doing, "Dacari/Son"?

I've always wanted to be financially successful. Many of my peers and associates have the same desire. We wake up, and work our asses off to achieve some high level of success.

Yet, many of us ignore the toll it takes on our personal lives and relationships. From 2014 to the present, I travel between 10-14 days out of each month for work. What many fail to realize about this travel life is that it takes a toll on every aspect of your life. When you travel, your body is in a constant state of adjustment to different food, water, accommodations, climate, work expectations, and time zones. Any kind of steady, healthy patterns of sleep, exercise, nutrition, and relationships are interrupted, and it's rough to try to keep up with good health habits somewhere else.

Life keeps moving on in your home despite your schedule. When you're trying to pack with your mind on the journey ahead, the family may feel your absence even while you are still home. Arriving home can be worse as you'd love to be welcomed home with excitement, while the one who has been at home may want nothing more than to be relieved of the additional responsibilities he or she has been shouldering. This is when things started to get interesting in my marriage.

When my wife and I decided to leave Nashville for Atlanta, she expected just that. She had an expectation that I would divorce myself from Nashville and begin a new life in Atlanta. She was right, however, as noted earlier, I was ready to leave. I was hurt by my job and that church system, but I was conflicted. I had been working in the non-profit sector for four years, and I knew it would be difficult to change careers without starting over. Remember: I wanted to be in a company where financial growth and opportunity was possible.

Though it wasn't happening with the church, I knew that going backwards was not an option, so I stayed. My pastor and mentor created the perfect system for me. He allowed me to live in a different city, and still work and be compensated at the same. Honestly, it was a lot more flexible and less demanding. Not only that, this gave me more chances to find opportunities in the mass media field. Only having to really work two weeks out of the month was a blessing…at least I thought.

My wife was not opposed to the traveling schedule, but the tension was in the length. I thought, "well, I'm only here 14 days," but I didn't understand the strain. It's how Lynne Silva-Breen puts it when she states, "Human relationships need physical proximity, regular conversation, shared patterns of caregiving, humor, health, and equality to thrive." Trying to have achieve all of these, while traveling for a job, is like trying to juggle three balls when all you've ever managed was two. My wife needed to feel secure, not necessarily just financially, but she also need to feel emotionally secure. We were not struggling financially, but emotionally, we were drowning, and I didn't see it, understand it, or catch on to it.

An emotional need "is a craving that, when satisfied, leaves you with a feeling of happiness and contentment, and, when unsatisfied, leaves you with a feeling of unhappiness and frustration," says clinical psychologist and author, Dr. Willard F. Harley, Jr. His numerous books on marriage and relationships include *His Needs, Her Needs* which focuses on the needs of men and women and shows husbands and wives how to satisfy those needs in their spouses.

According to Harley, "satisfying your own emotional needs means putting your spouse's desires ahead of your own." And this is what I struggled with: learning to put my wife's needs ahead of mine. In my pursuit of success, I became selfish, and began to believe my wife wasn't supporting me and didn't care about my wishes. It wasn't that she didn't support me; it was that we were having an emotional drought in the relationship, and I couldn't see it, so I struggled to fix it.

And you can't heal what you don't reveal, right?

After a few months of traveling back and forth between Atlanta and Nashville, things started to settle. We were communicating a little better, but the traveling was still an issue. My wife and I would argue often. Every trip I felt that she was nagging, but all she wanted was her husband. The more she stated her feelings, the more I rebel, and begin to check out...to check out of the marriage. And boom: two important dates changed everything.

On December 17, 2014, I had come home from Nashville on a mission. I came home to share with my wife that I was ready to separate. We had talked about it before, but I had enough. I was angry, and something needed to be done. When I arrived home, I didn't speak; my mind was on one thing: SEPARATION. After 10 minutes of silence, she finally spoke, and gave me a gift bag. I thought to myself, *why would she want to give me a gift; we've been arguing all week?* I didn't want anything from her but a SEPARATION.

Nevertheless, I opened the bag, and saw a lot of Atlanta Falcons paraphernalia, but the clothing, particularly the socks, were those fit for a child. When I asked, who we were giving the clothes to, she said "ours." Immediately, I went from great sadness-to confusion-to happiness-to "oh shit!" My wife shared with me *that I was about to become a father.* All of the emotions surrounding a SEPARATION were out of the door. My focus was centered on making my marriage work, and being a great father to my child. I agreed to start counseling, and we went for it.

Then...

I remember an email I received shortly after this announcement that said, "Dacari per our conversation, regarding your employment status, your last paycheck will be December 26, 2014."

Let me give more context.

When my pastor and I discussed my move to Atlanta, we talked about me transitioning into a new role with a larger organization that he had taken over. However, that move wouldn't take place until July/August of 2015. Yet, we would have a plan in the meantime to keep me employed until that move. However, that email didn't state those plans. It was simple: you will have to wait it out until July; find some other work to do until then. As you can imagine, the stress level skyrocketed.

How am I going to tell my wife that I won't have a job, and we're expecting a child? What am I going to do?

So, I kept it to myself. I internalized it all and worked through it. I never shared it with my wife, because I was afraid to. My wife already felt some sort of way about the organization based on what she saw me dealing with. She was no longer a fan of the church or the system. As a matter of fact, she had warned me that they could hurt me again, and they were not to be trusted. Therefore, why would I share with her that she was right? The same organization that I'm traveling back and forth for is giving me an exit plan! The organization that I'm seeking affirmation from, that would give me the success I wanted, was saying my departure was near. How could I share that with my wife… the organization that, in her mind, was taking me away from the family? No way! I was not going to reveal that, and I didn't.

Nevertheless, after internalizing this and working through it alone for a while, I reached out to my pastor, and he agreed to keep me employed until we worked out the other position in Atlanta.

Why Is Dacari Here?

Over the course of three years, I started to hear the reference, "Bishop's Boy." This was relative to the relationship I developed with my Bishop. He and I have a relationship that many envy, because they don't understand it. *How is it that Dacari can live in another state and collect a paycheck? He's rarely here, but somehow Bishop keeps him around, and he's an executive... how is this possible?*

In Cy Wakeman's book *The Reality-Based Rules of the Workplace*, she talks about an employee's value or what they bring to the organization. She uses this formula:

Employee Value = Current Performance (How am I doing today?) + Future Potential (Am I ready for what's next?) – (3x) Emotional Expensiveness (Am I worth it?) In essence, this metric includes what an employee brings to the organization now and into the future and weighs that against the true cost of the employee...the cost in addition to salary and benefits.

Thus, to answer the question of Dacari's why: I add immense value to the organization. I've done more for our organization while away than I did when I was present. Despite these facts, the tension still remained, and remains.

As I began to assimilate into the new role with the larger organization, I began to hear the concerns of those who were currently working. *Why is Dacari here? He's not necessary to what we're doing! We don't need him!* I thought, *here we go with this again.* All I ever want to do is be an asset to any space I occupy. I never asked for the dislike or disdain from the organizations, but it happens.

One of the areas I was supposed to work in was marketing and branding. This is one of my strongest areas, and I know what I'm doing. However, I was never included in the conversations regarding that. I was mainly invited in once decisions were made. There were few times that I was invited to share the "how's," and "why's." And when I did, many of those decisions were seldom used. I felt excluded, and again not valued. *One of the hardest things for Millennials is to have knowledge or expertise in an area, and we're rarely granted the opportunity to share.*

Between both organizations and their lack of understanding my value, it created more internal tension within while simultaneously causing outward expressions that translated into emotional abusive to my wife.

I was angry often, didn't want to spend time with my wife, or any of my friends. I wanted to be left alone. I found myself searching and applying for jobs so that I could get out of that system. I applied to over 30 jobs and even spoke to job recruiters via LinkedIn but had no luck. I felt like a first-time graduate again…looking for a promising job with rewards. Honestly, I was lost.

It was at this point that I said to my wife. *"Hey Lar, I think I'm depressed."*

I Think I'm Depressed

As we sat in the kitchen discussing the eminent arrival of our child, I became frighten by the idea of it all. I didn't like my job, I was becoming a terrible husband, and I was uncertain about my future as a father. I told my wife that I was depressed, and she advised that I should get counseling.

Kim Eisenberg, a prominent consultant in speaking about depression and careers, asks and answers a prominent question in which I agree with,

So why are there so many people who are simultaneously depressed *and* in career transition? Not to be overly simplistic, but this stuff is hard! If you're a human being with a soul, it's going to wear on you. Whether it's a toxic work environment, being long-term unemployed, financial instability, or any other flavor of angst, these situations takes a heavy toll.

When you're simultaneously depressed and trying to make a career change, voluntary or involuntary, the combination can be immobilizing. And the longer it drags on, the harder it is to just "bootstrap" yourself out of it. (Honestly, most people can't bootstrap themselves out of it no matter the circumstances.) So many of my clients are bright, talented, and desperately want to change their situations. By all rational accounts, they are very motivated. But as soon as it's time for them to do energy-intensive work (i.e. things other than applying for jobs online), they stall out. Often to their own shock and dismay.

Career transition requires a lot of heavy lifting, and in order to do it effectively, you have to be in reasonably good mental health. If you're depressed, it's damn near impossible. Enter **THE BIG PROBLEM**: for most folks in this situation, their depression isn't going to really lift until they're fully employed in a meaningful position. But it's really friggin' hard to make a successful transition when depressed.

Once I realized the career transition wouldn't happen right away, *I sought help.*

And according to National Institute of Mental Health, "nearly 15 million American adults, or about 6.7% of the U.S. population, age 18 and older, is affected with a major depression in a given year."

And I didn't want to sit on the couch...

In a *Psychology Today* article, I read,

On average, White Americans are two times more likely to go to counseling than their African American counterparts. This disparity isn't only because African Americans believe mental health services are expensive or costly, either. There is a stigma associated with going to therapy in the black community.

We are viewed as "crazy" or "weak" if you aren't able to handle issues that may arise in your life.

According to Monnica T. Williams, licensed clinical psychologist and Associate Director of the Center for Mental Health Disparities at the University of Louisville,

Studies have found that, "among blacks, who were already mental health consumers, over a third felt that mild depression or anxiety would be considered *crazy* in their social circles. That same study also found that" a fourth of those consumers believed that discussing mental illness would not even be appropriate among family.

If you can't go to a counselor about a crippling depression and you can't talk to your family about it, *what can you do?*

Again, this was not my first bout with a counselor, however, it was the second time talking to a counselor simultaneously about depression and marriage. This was tough. I knew I was depressed, but I couldn't understand, at the time, how it was affecting my marriage. I knew that I was slowly checking out of my marriage, but I didn't understand how to stop it. I figured that I would eventually snap out of it, but I slowly digressed. Rather than share my thoughts about depression, I would often state to my therapist my marital concerns. I would talk about how uncertain I was about marriage and the institution. I was wrestling deeply with the "why" of marriage. *I didn't want to remain married.*

"The partner who isn't depressed may also feel cheated," says Dan Jones, PhD, director of the Counseling and Psychological

Services Center at Appalachian State University in Boone, N.C. "That's understandable," he says, "because the depressed partner is typically not much fun. Most people fall in love because they are enjoying each other's company and having fun together,"

My wife and I had a lot of fun together prior to this bout with depression. We were what many would call the life of the party. People enjoyed our presence. Yet, overtime, no one enjoyed my presence as much. I wasn't much fun—I preferred to stay in the house. I preferred to be alone. Being in isolation was my happy place. Who knew it would eventually become more destructive.

As Jones continues, he furthers his point by stating more of my truth:

The depressed person will [often] give the impression he doesn't care. It's hard to feel intimate with someone [who looks like he does not care]; there is often a loss of interest in sex by the depressed person which further strains the relationship.

Listen, this was real. I have friends who say, "I don't care what's happening in my life, I will never not want sex." Well, the depressed mind changed my whole perspective on this issue. I became uninterested in intimacy. I'm very affectionate, and a passionate person, but my wife didn't receive any of this attention. When I sought affection, I turned to pornography. I fixated my eyes and mind of Instagram models. I created fantasies in my mind, and lived in that space as long as I could, until I felt bad.

Another issue we dealt with was distance. As the article notes, if the depression persists for months or years, both partners can feel the distance between them widening. Over the course of two and half years, we lost what made our relationship special: friendship and intimacy. I no longer wanted it, and I was done with it all.

Though I had emotionally checked out of the marriage, I was still present. So, my wife, being a champion for marriage, decided that we needed to seek counseling *together*.

In addition to other perspectives, Jones believes, seeing a therapist together can give a couple valuable perspective. "The therapist mediates; it's not a blaming session, but rather the therapist helps the depressed person recognize they are contributing to [the problem]. If they improve the depression, they could improve the marriage."

We saw four marital counselors over the course of three and a half years…two of which were great. The challenge again was I did not want to do the work required. I honestly, didn't know why we were there. My wife thought I was actually working to gain back our connection, but I was working to see how we could co-exist, and eventually co-parent.

The Sequel: My Son

My wife began having bad cramps on that Friday. We went to the hospital, and they sent us back home —she wasn't ready. All day Saturday I watched her walk back and forth in pain. I can only imagine that's how it must have felt to watch her husband lose his way. I have constantly wondered how massive the strength of a woman is. To carry a child almost ten months, watch your food intake, watch your body transform—then boom: your child is here, and now you have to care for yourself and a little being.

How could I stay depressed knowing that God had given me what many have yearned and prayed for?

Well, according to hopexchange.com:

- There are about 4.4 million confirmed pregnancies in the U.S. every year.

- 900,000 to 1 million of those end in pregnancy losses EVERY year.

- More than 500,000 pregnancies each year end in miscarriage (occurring during the first 20 weeks).

- Approximately 26,000 end in stillbirth (considered stillbirth after 20 weeks)

- Approximately 19,000 end in infant death during the first month.

- Approximately 39,000 end in infant death during the first year.

- Approximately 1 in 4 pregnancies end in miscarriage; some estimates are as high as 1 in 3. If you include loss that occurs before a positive pregnancy test, some estimate that 40% of all conceptions result in loss.

- Approximately 75% of all miscarriages occur in the first trimester.

- An estimated 80% of all miscarriages are single miscarriages. The vast majority of women suffering one miscarriage can expect to have a normal pregnancy next time.

- An estimated 19% of the adult population has experienced the death of a child (this includes miscarriages through adult-aged children).

So again, with all of these facts, and statistics, how could I stay depressed? Not only were my career, bitterness with the institution of marriage, lack of friendships, leaving Nashville etc. a factor, but now, *I was afraid to be a father, because I wasn't sure if I could be one considering that mine was never present.*

I could write essays about the effects of an absent father, yet that wasn't the issue. *I was just afraid to BE.* I placed many expectations on myself. *Make sure you teach him this, have him to sit up this way, and talk like this.* I want my son to succeed just as bad as I want to breath. In essence, I created this sense of anxiety for myself; from my own insecurities birthed unrealistic expectations. Besides, he wasn't even born yet, and I had already beaten myself up.

On Sunday afternoon, we went back to the hospital, and waited the arrival of our son. Around 4:50am on Monday morning, August 17, 2015, to be exact, my precious son…my baby boy and my namesake arrived. Believe it or not, I didn't shed a tear. I was in awe and slightly tired. I was just happy that he made it safely, and everything was well.

It was our blessing; it was God's plan.

Over the course of a year, up until his first birthday we worked to keep our family together. There were some good days, and some very bad days. There were times when we laughed as we once did, and times were we both were ready to throw in the towel, the mouth piece, and every other component, but we didn't; *we stayed.* We kept going to counseling, even when our favorite counselor, who in our opinions was making progress, decided to move out of the state. While this was slightly damaging, we found another therapist, and we were sure he had it figured out.

After going to this guy for a few weeks, it became scary for us both. He was a marriage counselor, but he sought out and discovered that we needed personal/individual counseling. We both shared intimate moments with him, and when we returned, we found out certain truths about ourselves. My wife saw it working, and so did I, but I declined the invitation to go deeper. I didn't like discovering things about myself. It's weird, right? I could finally begin to heal, yet the idea of healing would remove the sympathy I was receiving. For me, to stay in darkness allowed me to be what I wanted. I liked the idea of pain. It felt good for people to say, "I'm praying for you," or "you can make it." Was it attention that I needed? No, I'm the baby of the family, I've always gotten and still get enough attention.

So, what was it?

Hebrew University psychological scientist Maya Tamir, and her colleagues, have been studying how people with depression regulate their emotions, and they may have an explanation for my acquaintance's paradoxical and forlorn lifestyle choices:

Emotional regulation is the process of changing one's current emotions into more desirable ones. We all do it all the time. It's well known and not all that surprising that depressed people have difficulty with emotion regulation, but Tamir believes that we have been looking at emotion dysregulation the wrong way. Specifically, we've been assuming that depression is linked to deficits in emotional regulation strategies, when in fact the problem may have to do with emotional regulation goals.

Was I regulating my emotions to sustain a sense of sadness?

As she continues, she believes that the problem may be more basic:

It may instead be that depressed people are choosing the wrong emotion regulation goal to begin with. That is… depressed people may be effective enough in regulating their emotions, but they may be choosing to regulate in a direction that reinforces their negative mood. This raises the possibility that depressed people are actually more motivated to experience unpleasant emotions like sadness, as strange as this sounds.

She then asks this question, then answers:

So why, if they prefer happiness, would they deliberately choose regulatory goals that undermine that happiness? One possibility, the scientists say, is that depressed people use emotion regulation to verify their emotional selves. In other words, sadness is more familiar to depressed people, so they are motivated to experience sadness as a way of reaffirming who they are. Depression is also closely tied to low self-esteem, and it may be that depressed people believe that they deserve to feel bad.

I slowly changed my thinking after reading this research. It wasn't that I liked pain or felt like I should enjoy this. *But I believed that I deserved to feel bad. You brought all of this on yourself,* I thought. *You should have been a man*, and told your wife the truth about your job, leaving Nashville, being afraid of fatherhood. You, Dacari…*you deserve to feel bad. It's all your fault*, and because of it, *you have to live with it.* So, I decided that I would stop going to counseling, and figure this thing out on my own.

It was my fault, and in my mind, no therapist could help me. Thus, as the earlier article stated, sometimes, the partner of a person with depression will feel responsible, and stick with the marriage even if they've become more of a caretaker than a spouse. My wife became a caretaker; she was caring for someone who didn't care for themselves. She was a hero. She cared. I didn't…and this went on for *years.* She was physically, and emotionally present, and I was emotionally and physically unavailable. And with anything, the strain of staying committed to a depressed partner gets tiring, and eventually that spouse will seek separation or divorce.

The Day She Stopped Wearing Her Ring

I walked in the master bathroom of our home one morning, after she'd left for work, looking for Q-tips, and I found something that startled me: my wife's engagement ring and two wedding bands were on the counter. Initially, I thought she left them by accident. Yet, after further investigating of the matter, it was no accident. After asking her about it, my wife said, "you don't want to be married, so why should I wear a wedding ring?"

Over the course of two and a half years, my marriage was on the decline. One of the most prominent reasons for my disconnection was the fact that I viewed my wife as the enemy. I no longer saw her as my friend. I saw her as a person trying to derail me from my dreams. I felt like my wife was no longer supportive of my desires and dreams. I saw my wife as a threat, and because of this, it created tension.

John Wilkinson wrote an article about spouses who used depression as a reason to leave. He states,

Depressed partners may refuse to face the inner pain that's wrecking their lives. Rather than seek treatment, they come to believe that it's the existing relationship that is ruining them. Their answer is often to leave and find happiness elsewhere."

I thought that escaping the marriage would solve the problem, but what I discovered was no matter where I went, I was still there.

He furthers this argument, and captures my emotions perfectly:

Talking about "inner pain" suggests despair or other unbearable hurt that demands an explanation and must be escaped as quickly as possible. Since depression is a condition that can vary from day to day, that active side of pain can be the driving motive. But there is another dimension of depression that can lead to the idea of escape as the answer. It's the one that causes depressed partners to say they're no longer in love and have never loved their partners. It's called *anhedonia*, the inability to feel pleasure or interest in anything.

For me, it was a kind of deadness. Rather than an excess of painful emotion, it was the lack of pain, the lack of feeling, that was the undercurrent of all the surface turmoil. I believed that the relationship was holding me back. It had become hollow, empty of the intensity I longed for. I could only find happiness and passion with someone else. It was the fantasy of the perfectly passionate mate that was a constant lure.

I believed that my marriage was holding me back. From what you ask? I thought I was being held back from my dreams, but that couldn't have been it, because I'm *still* searching for the dream. I thought she was no longer the one, and there was this other perfect person for me. I sought every reason possible on why I wanted to leave the marriage. Frankly, I was unhappy— not just with my wife, but mainly with myself, and she received the bulk of the blame for my own misery.

In Peter Kramer's insightful book, *Should You Leave,* he deals with many of these emotions.

As one of the dwindling number of psychiatrists who still practice psychotherapy, I often work with clients who are dissatisfied with their relationships. They want to know if leaving is the best thing to do. When I encounter someone, who is convinced that the marriage is dead, I always suspects depression or another mood disorder. I can sense that the person before me could well have an undiagnosed depression that has emptied him of all feeling. Anhedonia is the cause of the desire to leave to find a new, more intense life. His relationship feels loveless because he can hardly feel at all.

The problem is that the unaware depressive has such a high threshold of feeling that it takes extreme arousal to evoke excitement and passion. He can erupt with anger and rage because these are more violent emotions that stir him as little else does. Kramer says that these clients often believe that they're perfectly capable of feeling. After all, they can go out and have fun with friends. They can feel passionate with others who likely have no constraining relationships or might be seeking the same kind of escape. But they feel good precisely because these experiences offer exceptionally high levels of stimulation. They may also turn to addictive habits like recreational drugs, drinking, gambling or pornography for the same reason.

Fantasies of escaping into a life full of new intensity seem like the perfect answer to their inner emptiness.

My fantasies included the Atlanta Falcons, pornography, pain pills, and alcohol.

And I had so many demons...

As our relationship grew worse, I decided to move downstairs in our basement. I created more distance, and more space for destructive behaviors. I began exploring with pornography. And Dr. Gary Brooks, argues that,

Pornography floods the brain with dopamine and makes us feel good. Over time, as more dopamine is released, viewers can feel the effects of the feel-good dopamine less and less, which leads people to search for hardcore porn more often. For many, a porn habit can become a substitute for the feeling of happiness. As a viewer, self-medicates feelings of sadness with graphic sexual images and videos, they are missing out on building some real, amazing relationships with their spouse, friends, and/or community. In the end, no amount of pornography will take away life's problems. In fact, studies show that it will just become one of them. This became my issue, and I loved every moment of it. It was my relief, and one of my spaces for happiness.

In 2005, a study of 400 internet users displayed a significant link between porn use and loneliness. In an airbrushed and sterilized atmosphere, porn creates unrealistic expectations of physical love between two human beings— ones that *real* women and men could never match up to. This can naturally lead to unrealistic expectations and deep dissatisfaction for the porn viewer. Studies show that the more porn a person consumes, the harder it becomes for them to be aroused by a real person or a real relationship. As a result, many porn viewers start feeling like something's wrong with them— they don't know how to be turned on by a real person, much less form a real intimate connection with one. And that can result in harm to mental and emotional health.

At the end of the day, staying away from porn is worth it because going back to it, again and again, can quickly lead to feelings of anxiety, depression, and loneliness. It may satisfy for a few minutes, but what results afterward just isn't worth it.

This was the start of the fantasy, but it became deeper. In addition, I turned to alcohol and pain pills. Every night, I would drink three to four glasses of bourbon and wash them down with *lore tabs* or percocet. I loved the feeling of being drunk and high. *It took the feelings of inadequacies away.*

Scripture tells us, in Proverbs 13:12, that "a hope deferred makes the heart sick." My heart was sick, and I was praying that it stopped. According to the <u>National Institute on Alcohol Abuse and Alcoholism</u> (NIAAA), "depression can arise and increase during a battle with alcoholism. This increase in depression can then lead to more drinking, thus perpetuating this cycle from the other angle."

According to a study published in <u>Addiction</u>,

Individuals dealing with alcohol use disorder or depression are at double the risk of developing the other condition." And this was not simply a correlation, as the study concluded that alcohol use disorders and depression have a causal relationship. There were links found between the neurophysiological and metabolic changes brought about by alcohol abuse and the mechanisms for depression to occur. The study concluded that abuse of alcohol puts an individual at a significantly greater risk to develop depression than that of a person who is not abusing the substance.

Therefore, it is clear that alcohol abuse can induce depression, and depression can also induce alcohol abuse. This relationship can be cyclical as well, and an individual can get caught going back and forth between abusing alcohol and then using alcohol to try to quell the resulting depression. It can be an extremely challenging set of co-occurring disorders to address.

I was sick, and no one knew. I was, what my therapist called, a high functioning depressive. I was still performing at a high level at work, and many of my friends never saw this. Yet, my wife was experiencing it all. My wife caught me several times loading up on alcohol prior to driving to Nashville for work. I would drive three and a half hours back and forth sipping on Alcohol. While so selfish and dangerous, at the time, it didn't matter; I just didn't care. I became a cancer in my home. There were so many nights I kissed and loved on my son and he didn't know that I was high and drunk. I was empty, and I needed so much help.

The pain pills not only eased my body, they helped to create other desires and fantasies. There were many days when I didn't know where I was, and I was happy with that.

According to Psycom.net,

The relationship between opioid abuse and depression is bi-directional, meaning that suffering from one increases the risk of the other. Opioid abuse is defined as using a prescription opioid for non-medical reasons or using it longer or in greater amounts than what was prescribed by a doctor, and opioid abuse has been linked to higher rates of depression, anxiety, and bipolar disorders. But some research suggests that simply using prescription opioids can put one at higher risk or depression. In one study at St. Louis University, researchers found that 10% of over 100,000 patients prescribed opioids developed depression after using the medications for over a month. These patients were taking the medication for ailments such as back pain, headaches, arthritis, etc. and had not received a diagnosis of depression prior to treatment.

It's not important to note where I was getting my opioids from; the mere fact that I could get them so easily was quite troubling. Nevertheless, though this started as a nightly habit, I began taking them throughout the day. I walked around stoned, and people didn't notice. I would be around family members, even driving my son back and forth to school high. I loved the feeling of being numb. It became my norm.

I'm Out

I no longer knew if my wife was the one. I didn't trust her with me anymore. I was uncertain if she knew who I was. I wanted out, and I headed for the door. I sat downstairs in despair, lonely, and frightened that I would eventually die due to my destructive behavior. Therefore, versus working through my illness with my wife, I decided to go at it alone. *So, I moved out.*

I thought my home was toxic. I viewed my environment as unsafe. I was tired of seeing my wife cry, and my son confused. In essence, I ran. I ran from the greatest responsibility God had given me. I prayed for a wife, a son, a family, and God granted me these things, yet I fled. I left hoping to recover on my own and my wife hated this. She felt alone, ashamed, guilty, and betrayed.

But, I couldn't see any of these things, because I was focused on myself. It was about what Dacari wanted. I wanted to feel free, and whole, and I didn't think I could achieve it with my wife. I had already left her emotionally, and now I was physically gone. I saw it as a step of recovery, but my wife saw it as the finale.

According to writer Heather Gray,

When someone is depressed, they often seem so immobilized and frozen. It makes partners want to jump all in and give 110%. It's hard to ignore that impulse to rescue. It can feel impossible to bear witness to a loved one's pain, sadness, and suffering. It makes sense that you want to leap in to save your partner from this melancholy. In that moment, witnessing that pain, you're willing to do anything to bring relief.

My wife tried everything she could to help me. She found counselors, she stops complaining about my travel. She allowed me to be. She gave me the space needed to recover even when I left the home. She stayed present and available.

As I stayed away, and detached from my marriage, I begin to notice that I wasn't getting better; I was just becoming bitter. I started to resent my wife even more. I really believed she didn't know who I was, and what I was trying to accomplish. I blamed her for my own demise. This freedom to become, the freedom to be was not what I thought. I thought that I would arrive at this special place called destiny, and I would return back to my wife and son. I didn't know if she was still the one, but I knew I could figure it out if I had more time with myself and no responsibility of being a husband. Yes...the responsibility of being a husband was weighty. I didn't want that responsibility anymore. I just wanted to find my old self again, and once I did that, things would be back to normal.

It's so easy to think that a man can manage or even control a woman's emotional state. I did whatever I wanted to do, and expected my wife to hang around and be there. I excluded her out of every part of my life. I no longer invited her to the Falcons games with me, no happy hours, no Instagram photos, no special anniversary gifts. *I quit on my wife, as I did on my Bishop.* I ran like Forrest Gump, and I didn't look back. I poured thirteen years of friendship, and love down the drain, and I was unaware of my actions. It seems so simple in my mind: you, get you better, then you can go back and get your family. *I thought I had it figured out.* I thought I knew what I was doing, until I didn't know what I was doing.

My wife and I are now divorced, and we're both doing our best to construct a new normal.

My ex-wife did everything possible to save our marriage. She practically begged me to come back home. Even up until the last minute of signing our divorce papers, she asked me if I was sure. I didn't respond with a "yes" or a "no," but my uncertainty was enough for her to go through with it.

Now, I feel ashamed, embarrassed, guilty, and unworthy of love. I often wonder to myself, *what happened? How did it get so far? Why didn't I want to work through this?*

Parts of me gives this answer: I didn't have enough emotional energy to dedicate to it. I thought that maybe it was someone else that was designed to be with me. Being a husband was hard. I no longer liked the institution of marriage. I just didn't want it. I'm not sure if any of these answers are correct or not, but what I know now is this: yes, *I'm Out*—out of answers and out of my own way.

Part Five:

All Eyez on Me

Will I survive, will I die? Come on let's picture the possibility.
Was hyper as a kid, cold as a teenager
On my mobile calling big shots on the scene major
Make sure your eyes is on the meal ticket
Get your money motherfucker let's get rich and we'll kick it
All eyez on me!
-Tupac

"Hey, Big Head..."

This is a term used when someone "shoots their shot at you" (They are interested in dating, courting, or even potentially marrying you). While this isn't applicable for this subheading, I think it's important to note that this is what depression did to me. It took its shot, and we've been on and off again for the past thirteen years. Yet, I'm believing that we will divorce by the end of this book. It's had a great impact on my life, but it's time to let "big head" go. Let's see what happens when depression invades your life.

In the following few pages, you will see information regarding a study done by Harvard on depression and its effect on the brain. This is highly important to the conversation. Please pay attention to the graphs, and attempt to understand its findings. I'm hoping those of us who are affected by depression will win this battle.

For the next few pages, I have included valuable research and information provided publicly to us from Harvard Health Publishing at Harvard Medical School. For even more information, you can visit www.health.harvard.edu:

Depression results from a chemical imbalance, but that figure of speech doesn't capture how complex the disease is. Research suggests that depression doesn't spring from simply having too much or too little of certain brain chemicals. Rather, there are many possible causes of depression, including faulty mood regulation by the brain, genetic vulnerability, stressful life events, medications, and medical problems. It's believed that several of these forces interact to bring on depression.

To be sure, chemicals are involved in this process, but it is not a simple matter of one chemical being too low and another too high. Rather, many chemicals are involved, working both inside and outside nerve cells. There are millions, even billions, of chemical reactions that make up the dynamic system that is responsible for your mood, perceptions, and how you experience life.

With this level of complexity, you can see how two people might have similar symptoms of depression, but the problem on the inside, and therefore what treatments will work best, may be entirely different.

Researchers have learned much about the biology of depression. They've identified genes that make individuals more vulnerable to low moods and influence how an individual responds to drug therapy. One day, these discoveries should lead to better, more individualized treatment (see "From the lab to your medicine cabinet"), but that is likely to be years away. And while researchers know more now than ever before about how the brain regulates mood, their understanding of the biology of depression is far from complete.

What follows is an overview of the current understanding of the major factors believed to play a role in depression.

The Brain's Impact on Depression

Popular lore has it that emotions reside in the heart. Science, though, tracks the seat of your emotions to the brain. Certain areas of the brain help regulate mood. Researchers believe that — more important than levels of specific brain chemicals — nerve cell connections, nerve cell growth, and the functioning of nerve circuits have a major impact on depression. Still, their understanding of the neurological underpinnings of mood is incomplete.

Regions That Affect Mood

Increasingly sophisticated forms of brain imaging — such as positron emission tomography (PET), single-photon emission computed tomography (SPECT), and functional magnetic resonance imaging (fMRI) — permit a much closer look at the working brain than was possible in the past. An fMRI scan, for example, can track changes that take place when a region of the brain responds during various tasks. A PET or SPECT scan can map the brain by measuring the distribution and density of neurotransmitter receptors in certain areas.

Use of this technology has led to a better understanding of which brain regions regulate mood and how other functions, such as memory, may be affected by depression. Areas that play a significant role in depression are the amygdala, the thalamus, and the hippocampus (see Figure 1).

Research shows that the hippocampus is smaller in some depressed people. For example, in one fMRI study published in *The Journal of Neuroscience*, investigators studied 24 women who had a history of depression. On average, the hippocampus was 9% to 13% smaller in depressed women compared with those who were not depressed. The more bouts of depression a woman had, the smaller the hippocampus. Stress, which plays a role in depression, may be a key factor here, since experts believe stress can suppress the production of new neurons (nerve cells) in the hippocampus.

Researchers are exploring possible links between sluggish production of new neurons in the hippocampus and low moods. An interesting fact about antidepressants supports this theory. These medications immediately boost the concentration of chemical messengers in the brain (neurotransmitters). Yet people typically don't begin to feel better for several weeks or longer. Experts have long wondered why, if depression were primarily the result of low levels of neurotransmitters, people don't feel better as soon as levels of neurotransmitters increase.

The answer may be that mood only improves as nerves grow and form new connections, a process that takes weeks. In fact, animal studies have shown that antidepressants do spur the growth and enhanced branching of nerve cells in the hippocampus. So, the theory holds, the real value of these medications may be in generating new neurons (a process called neurogenesis), strengthening nerve cell connections, and improving the exchange of information between nerve circuits. If that's the case, medications could be developed that specifically promote neurogenesis, with the hope that patients would see quicker results than with current treatments.

Figure 1: Areas of the brain affected by depression.

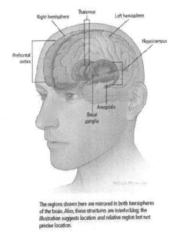

The regions shown here are mirrored in both hemispheres of the brain. Also, these structures are interlocking; the illustration suggests location and relative region but not precise location.

Amygdala: The amygdala is part of the limbic system, a group of structures deep in the brain that's associated with emotions such as anger, pleasure, sorrow, fear, and sexual arousal. The amygdala is activated when a person recalls emotionally charged memories, such as a frightening situation. Activity in the amygdala is higher when a person is sad or clinically depressed. This increased activity continues even after recovery from depression.

Thalamus: The thalamus receives most sensory information and relays it to the appropriate part of the cerebral cortex, which directs high-level functions such as speech, behavioral reactions, movement, thinking, and learning. Some research suggests that bipolar disorder may result from problems in the thalamus, which helps link sensory input to pleasant and unpleasant feelings.

Hippocampus: The hippocampus is part of the limbic system and has a central role in processing long-term memory and recollection. Interplay between the hippocampus and the amygdala might account for the adage "once bitten, twice shy." It is this part of the brain that registers fear when you are confronted by a barking, aggressive dog, and the memory of such an experience may make you wary of dogs you come across later in life. The hippocampus is smaller in some depressed people, and research suggests that ongoing exposure to stress hormone impairs the growth of nerve cells in this part of the brain.

Nerve Cell Communication

The ultimate goal in treating the biology of depression is to improve the brain's ability to regulate mood. We now know that neurotransmitters are not the *only* important part of the machinery. But let's not diminish their importance either. They are deeply involved in how nerve cells communicate with one another. And they are a component of brain function that we can often influence to good ends.

Neurotransmitters are chemicals that relay messages from neuron to neuron. An antidepressant medication tends to increase the concentration of these substances in the spaces between neurons (the synapses). In many cases, this shift appears to give the system enough of a nudge so that the brain can do its job better.

How the System Works

If you trained a high-powered microscope on a slice of brain tissue, you might be able to see a loosely braided network of neurons that send and receive messages. While every cell in the body has the capacity to send and receive signals, neurons are specially designed for this function. Each neuron has a cell body containing the structures that any cell needs to thrive. Stretching out from the cell body are short, branchlike fibers called dendrites and one longer, more prominent fiber called the axon.

A combination of electrical and chemical signals allows communication within and between neurons. When a neuron becomes activated, it passes an electrical signal from the cell body down the axon to its end (known as the axon terminal), where chemical messengers called neurotransmitters are stored. The signal releases certain neurotransmitters into the space between that neuron and the dendrite of a neighboring neuron. That space is called a synapse. As the concentration of a neurotransmitter rises in the synapse, neurotransmitter molecules begin to bind with receptors embedded in the membranes of the two neurons (see Figure 2).

The release of a neurotransmitter from one neuron can activate or inhibit a second neuron. If the signal is activating, or excitatory, the message continues to pass farther along that particular neural pathway. If it is inhibitory, the signal will be suppressed. The neurotransmitter also affects the neuron that released it. Once the first neuron has released a certain amount of the chemical, a feedback mechanism (controlled by that neuron's receptors) instructs the neuron to stop pumping out the neurotransmitter and start bringing it back into the cell. This process is called reabsorption or reuptake. Enzymes break down the remaining neurotransmitter molecules into smaller particles.

When the System Falters

Brain cells usually produce levels of neurotransmitters that keep senses, learning, movements, and moods perking along. But in some people who are severely depressed or manic, the complex systems that accomplish this go awry. For example, receptors may be oversensitive or insensitive to a specific neurotransmitter, causing their response to its release to be excessive or inadequate. Or a message might be weakened if the originating cell pumps out too little of a neurotransmitter or if an overly efficient reuptake mops up too much before the molecules have the chance to bind to the receptors on other neurons. Any of these system faults could significantly affect mood.

Kinds of Neurotransmitters

Scientists have identified many different neurotransmitters. Here is a description of a few believed to play a role in depression:

- Acetylcholine enhances memory and is involved in learning and recall.

- Serotonin helps regulate sleep, appetite, and mood and inhibits pain. Research supports the idea that some depressed people have reduced serotonin transmission. Low levels of a serotonin byproduct have been linked to a higher risk for suicide.

- Norepinephrine constricts blood vessels, raising blood pressure. It may trigger anxiety and be involved in some types of depression. It also seems to help determine motivation and reward.

- Dopamine is essential to movement. It also influences motivation and plays a role in how a person perceives reality. Problems in dopamine transmission have been associated with psychosis, a severe form of distorted thinking characterized by hallucinations or delusions. It's also involved in the brain's reward system, so it is thought to play a role in substance abuse.

- Glutamate is a small molecule believed to act as an excitatory neurotransmitter and to play a role in bipolar disorder and schizophrenia. Lithium carbonate, a well-known mood stabilizer used to treat bipolar disorder, helps prevent damage to neurons in the brains of rats exposed to high levels of glutamate. Other animal research suggests that lithium might stabilize glutamate reuptake, a mechanism that may explain how the drug smooths out the highs of mania and the lows of depression in the long term.

- Gamma-aminobutyric acid (GABA) is an amino acid that researchers believe acts as an inhibitory neurotransmitter. It is thought to help quell anxiety.

Figure 2: How neurons communicate

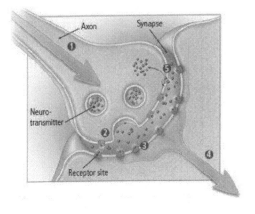

An electrical signal travels down the axon.

Chemical neurotransmitter molecules are released.

The neurotransmitter molecules bind to receptor sites.

The signal is picked up by the second neuron and is either passed along or halted.

The signal is also picked up by the first neuron, causing reuptake, the process by which the cell that released the neurotransmitter takes back some of the remaining molecules

Genes' Effect on Mood

Every part of your body, including your brain, is controlled by genes. Genes make proteins that are involved in biological processes. Throughout life, different genes turn on and off, so that — in the best case — they make the right proteins at the right time. But if the genes get it wrong, they can alter your biology in a way that results in your mood becoming unstable. In a genetically vulnerable person, any stress (a missed deadline at work or a medical illness, for example) can then push this system off balance.

Mood is affected by dozens of genes, and as our genetic endowments differ, so do our depressions. The hope is that as researchers pinpoint the genes involved in mood disorders and better understand their functions, treatment can become more individualized and more successful. Patients would receive the best medication for their type of depression.

Another goal of gene research, of course, is to understand how, exactly, biology makes certain people vulnerable to depression. For example, several genes influence the stress response, leaving us more or less likely to become depressed in response to trouble.

Perhaps the easiest way to grasp the power of genetics is to look at families. It is well known that depression and bipolar disorder run in families. The strongest evidence for this comes from the research on bipolar disorder. Half of those with bipolar disorder have a relative with a similar pattern of mood fluctuations. Studies of identical twins, who share a genetic blueprint, show that if one twin has bipolar disorder, the other has a 60% to 80% chance of developing it, too. These numbers don't apply to fraternal twins, who — like other biological siblings — share only about half of their genes. If one fraternal twin has bipolar disorder, the other has a 20% chance of developing it.

The evidence for other types of depression is more subtle, but it is real. A person who has a first-degree relative who suffered major depression has an increase in risk for the condition of 1.5% to 3% over normal.

One important goal of genetics research — and this is true throughout medicine — is to learn the specific function of each gene. This kind of information will help us figure out how the interaction of biology and environment leads to depression in some people but not others.

Temperament Shapes Behavior

Genetics provides one perspective on how resilient you are in the face of difficult life events. But you don't need to be a geneticist to understand yourself. Perhaps a more intuitive way to look at resilience is by understanding your temperament. Temperament — for example, how excitable you are or whether you tend to withdraw from or engage in social situations — is determined by your genetic inheritance and by the experiences you've had during the course of your life. Some people are able to make better choices in life once they appreciate their habitual reactions to people and to life events.

Cognitive psychologists point out that your view of the world and, in particular, your unacknowledged assumptions about how the world works also influence how you feel. You develop your viewpoint early on and learn to automatically fall back on it when loss, disappointment, or rejection occurs. For example, you may come to see yourself as unworthy of love, so you avoid getting involved with people rather than risk losing a relationship. Or you may be so self-critical that you can't bear the slightest criticism from others, which can slow or block your career progress.

Yet while temperament or world view may have a hand in depression, neither is unchangeable. Therapy and medications can shift thoughts and attitudes that have developed over time.

Stressful Life Events

At some point, nearly everyone encounters stressful life events: the death of a loved one, the loss of a job, an illness, or a relationship spiraling downward. Some must cope with the early loss of a parent, violence, or sexual abuse. While not everyone who faces, these stresses develop a mood disorder — in fact, most do not — stress plays an important role in depression.

As the previous section explained, your genetic makeup influences how sensitive you are to stressful life events. When genetics, biology, and stressful life situations come together, depression can result.

Stress has its own physiological consequences. It triggers a chain of chemical reactions and responses in the body. If the stress is short-lived, the body usually returns to normal. But when stress is chronic or the system gets stuck in overdrive, changes in the body and brain can be long-lasting.

How Stress Affects the Body

Stress can be defined as an automatic physical response to any stimulus that requires you to adjust to change. Every real or perceived threat to your body triggers a cascade of stress hormones that produces physiological changes. We all know the sensations: your heart pounds, muscles tense, breathing quickens, and beads of sweat appear. This is known as the stress response.

The stress response starts with a signal from the part of your brain known as the hypothalamus. The hypothalamus joins the pituitary gland and the adrenal glands to form a trio known as the hypothalamic-pituitary-adrenal (HPA) axis, which governs a multitude of hormonal activities in the body and may play a role in depression as well.

When a physical or emotional threat looms, the hypothalamus secretes corticotropin-releasing hormone (CRH), which has the job of rousing your body. Hormones are complex chemicals that carry messages to organs or groups of cells throughout the body and trigger certain responses. CRH follows a pathway to your pituitary gland, where it stimulates the secretion of adrenocorticotropic hormone (ACTH), which pulses into your bloodstream. When ACTH reaches your adrenal glands, it prompts the release of cortisol.

The boost in cortisol readies your body to fight or flee. Your heart beats faster — up to five times as quickly as normal — and your blood pressure rises. Your breath quickens as your body takes in extra oxygen. Sharpened senses, such as sight and hearing, make you more alert.

CRH also affects the cerebral cortex, part of the amygdala, and the brainstem. It is thought to play a major role in coordinating your thoughts and behaviors, emotional reactions, and involuntary responses. Working along a variety of neural pathways, it influences the concentration of neurotransmitters throughout the brain. Disturbances in hormonal systems, therefore, may well affect neurotransmitters, and vice versa.

Normally, a feedback loop allows the body to turn off "fight-or-flight" defenses when the threat passes. In some cases, though, the floodgates never close properly, and cortisol levels rise too often or simply stay high. This can contribute to problems such as high blood pressure, immune suppression, asthma, and possibly depression.

Studies have shown that people who are depressed or have dysthymia typically have increased levels of CRH. Antidepressants and electroconvulsive therapy are both known to reduce these high CRH levels. As CRH levels return to normal, depressive symptoms recede. Research also suggests that trauma during childhood can negatively affect the functioning of CRH and the HPA axis throughout life.

Early Losses and Trauma

Certain events can have lasting physical, as well as emotional, consequences. Researchers have found that early losses and emotional trauma may leave individuals more vulnerable to depression later in life.

Childhood Losses. Profound early losses, such as the death of a parent or the withdrawal of a loved one's affection, may resonate throughout life, eventually expressing themselves as depression. When an individual is unaware of the wellspring of his or her illness, he or she can't easily move past the depression. Moreover, unless the person gains a conscious understanding of the source of the condition, later losses or disappointments may trigger its return.

The British psychiatrist John Bowlby focused on early losses in a number of landmark studies of monkeys. When he separated young monkeys from their mothers, the monkeys passed through predictable stages of a separation response. Their furious outbursts trailed off into despair, followed by apathetic detachment. Meanwhile, the levels of their stress hormones rose. Later investigators extended this research. One study found that the CRH system and HPA axis got stuck in overdrive in adult rodents that had been separated from their mothers too early in life. This held true whether or not the rats were purposely put under stress. Interestingly, antidepressants and electroconvulsive therapy relieve the symptoms of animals distressed by such separations.

The Role of Trauma. Traumas may also be indelibly etched on the psyche. A small but intriguing study in the *Journal of the American Medical Association* showed that women who were abused physically or sexually as children had more extreme stress responses than women who had not been abused. The women had higher levels of the stress hormones ACTH and cortisol, and their hearts beat faster when they performed stressful tasks, such as working out mathematical equations or speaking in front of an audience.

Many researchers believe that early trauma causes subtle changes in brain function that account for symptoms of depression and anxiety. The key brain regions involved in the stress response may be altered at the chemical or cellular level. Changes might include fluctuations in the concentration of neurotransmitters or damage to nerve cells. However, further investigation is needed to clarify the relationship between the brain, psychological trauma, and depression.

Seasonal affective disorder: when winter brings the blues

Many people feel sad when summer wanes, but some actually develop depression with the season's change. Known as seasonal affective disorder (SAD), this form of depression affects about 1% to 2% of the population, particularly women and young people.

SAD seems to be triggered by more limited exposure to daylight; typically it comes on during the fall or winter months and subsides in the spring. Symptoms are similar to general depression and include lethargy, loss of interest in once-pleasurable activities, irritability, inability to concentrate, and a change in sleeping patterns, appetite, or both.

To combat SAD, doctors suggest exercise, particularly outdoor activities during daylight hours. Exposing yourself to bright artificial light may also help. Light therapy, also called phototherapy, usually involves sitting close to a special light source that is far more intense than normal indoor light for 30 minutes every morning. The light must enter through your eyes to be effective; skin exposure has not been proven to work. Some people feel better after only one light treatment, but most people require at least a few days of treatment, and some need several weeks. You can buy boxes that emit the proper light intensity (10,000 lux) with a minimal amount of ultraviolet light without a prescription, but it is best to work with a professional who can monitor your response.

There are few side effects to light therapy, but you should be aware of the following potential problems:

- Mild anxiety, jitteriness, headaches, early awakening, or eyestrain can occur.

- There is evidence that light therapy can trigger a manic episode in people who are vulnerable.

- While there is no proof that light therapy can aggravate an eye problem, you should still discuss any eye disease with your doctor before starting light therapy. Likewise, since rashes can result, let your doctor know about any skin conditions.

- Some drugs or herbs (for example, St. John's wort) can make you sensitive to light.

- If light therapy isn't helpful, antidepressants may offer relief.

Medical problems

Certain medical problems are linked to lasting, significant mood disturbances. In fact, medical illnesses or medications may be at the root of up to 10% to 15% of all depressions.

Among the best-known culprits are two thyroid hormone imbalances. An excess of thyroid hormone (hyperthyroidism) can trigger manic symptoms. On the other hand, hypothyroidism, a condition in which your body produces too little thyroid hormone, often leads to exhaustion and depression.

Heart disease has also been linked to depression, with up to half of heart attack survivors reporting feeling blue and many having significant depression. Depression can spell trouble for heart patients: it's been linked with slower recovery, future cardiovascular trouble, and a higher risk of dying within about six months. Although doctors have hesitated to give heart patients older depression medications called tricyclic antidepressants because of their impact on heart rhythms, selective serotonin reuptake inhibitors seem safe for people with heart conditions.

The following medical conditions have also been associated with mood disorders:

- degenerative neurological conditions, such as multiple sclerosis, Parkinson's disease, Alzheimer's disease, and Huntington's disease
- stroke
- some nutritional deficiencies, such as a lack of vitamin B12

- other endocrine disorders, such as problems with the parathyroid or adrenal glands that cause them to produce too little or too much of particular hormones

- certain immune system diseases, such as lupus

- some viruses and other infections, such as mononucleosis, hepatitis, and HIV

- cancer

- erectile dysfunction in men.

When considering the connection between health problems and depression, an important question to address is which came first, the medical condition or the mood changes. There is no doubt that the stress of having certain illnesses can trigger depression. In other cases, depression precedes the medical illness and may even contribute to it. To find out whether the mood changes occurred on their own or as a result of the medical illness, a doctor carefully considers a person's medical history and the results of a physical exam.

If depression or mania springs from an underlying medical problem, the mood changes should disappear after the medical condition is treated. If you have hypothyroidism, for example, lethargy and depression often lift once treatment regulates the level of thyroid hormone in your blood. In many cases, however, the depression is an independent problem, which means that in order to be successful, treatment must address depression directly.

An Out-of-sync Body Clock May Underlie SAD and Other Mood Disorders

Research into one form of depression — seasonal affective disorder (SAD) — has uncovered another potential factor in mood disorders: an internal body clock that has gone awry.

Experts don't fully understand the cause of SAD, but a leading theory has been that the hormone melatonin plays a role. The brain secretes melatonin at night, so longer periods of darkness in the winter months may spur greater production of this hormone. Some researchers believe light therapy has been helpful in treating SAD because exposure to light artificially lengthens daytime and decreases melatonin production.

But another theory has emerged: that SAD stems, at least partly, from an out-of-sync body clock. The researchers who propose this idea suggest that light therapy works because it resets the body's internal clock.

Each of us has a biological clock that regulates the circadian (meaning "about a day") rhythm of sleeping and waking. This internal clock — which is located in a small bundle of brain cells called the suprachiasmatic nucleus and gradually becomes established during the first months of life — controls the daily ups and downs of biological patterns, including body temperature, blood pressure, and the release of hormones. Although the clock is largely self-regulating, it responds to several cues to keep it set properly, including light and melatonin production.

When researchers expose people to light at intervals that are at odds with the outside world, this resets the subjects' biological clocks to match the new light input. Likewise, melatonin affects the body clock. It's produced in a predictable daily rhythm by the pineal gland, with levels climbing after dark and ebbing after dawn. Scientists believe this daily light-sensitive pattern helps keep the sleep/wake cycle on track.

Beyond SAD

A case is being made that circadian rhythms influence other mood disorders as well. Studies have uncovered out-of-sync circadian rhythms among people with bipolar disorder, schizophrenia, borderline personality disorder, or night eating disorder.

Figure 3: Getting back in sync.

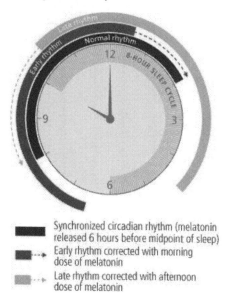

Synchronized circadian rhythm (melatonin released 6 hours before midpoint of sleep)

Early rhythm corrected with morning dose of melatonin

Late rhythm corrected with afternoon dose of melatonin

Medications

Sometimes, symptoms of depression or mania are a side effect of certain drugs, such as steroids or blood pressure medication. Be sure to tell your doctor or therapist what medications you take and when your symptoms began. A professional can help sort out whether a new medication, a change in dosage, or interactions with other drugs or substances might be affecting your mood.

Table 1 lists drugs that may affect mood. However, keep in mind the following:

- Researchers disagree about whether a few of these drugs — such as birth control pills or propranolol — affect mood enough to be a significant factor.

- Most people who take the medications listed will not experience mood changes, although having a family or personal history of depression may make you more vulnerable to such a change.

- Some of the drugs cause symptoms like malaise (a general feeling of being ill or uncomfortable) or appetite loss that may be mistaken for depression.

- Even if you are taking one of these drugs, your depression may spring from other sources.

Table 1: Medications that may cause depression
Antimicrobials, antibiotics, antifungals, and antivirals
acyclovir (Zovirax); alpha-interferons; cycloserine (Seromycin); ethambutol (Myambutol); levofloxacin (Levaquin); metronidazole (Flagyl); streptomycin; sulfonamides (AVC, Sultrin, Trysul); tetracycline
Heart and blood pressure drugs
beta blockers such as propranolol (Inderal), metoprolol (Lopressor, Toprol XL), atenolol (Tenormin); calcium-channel blockers such as verapamil (Calan, Isoptin, Verelan) and nifedipine (Adalat CC, Procardia XL); digoxin (Digitek, Lanoxicaps, Lanoxin); disopyramide (Norpace); methyldopa (Aldomet)
Hormones

anabolic steroids; danazol (Danocrine); glucocorticoids such as prednisone and adrenocorticotropic hormone; estrogens (e.g., Premarin, Prempro); oral contraceptives (birth control pills)

Tranquilizers, insomnia aids, and sedatives

barbiturates such as phenobarbital (Solfoton) and secobarbital (Seconal); benzodiazepines such as diazepam (Valium) and clonazepam (Klonopin)

Miscellaneous

acetazolamide (Diamox); antacids such as cimetidine (Tagamet) and ranitidine (Zantac); antiseizure drugs; baclofen (Lioresal); cancer drugs such as asparaginase (Elspar); cyclosporine (Neoral, Sandimmune); disulfiram (Antabuse); isotretinoin (Accutane); levodopa or L-dopa (Larodopa); metoclopramide (Octamide, Reglan); narcotic pain medications (e.g., codeine, Percodan, Demerol, morphine); withdrawal from cocaine or amphetamines

My hope is that all of the research and information, recently list, by these amazing experts, will aid you in understanding how the brain works, and the role depression plays in it.

It Didn't Start with You

I believe anything that's untreated will be repeated. I often wondered if depression was hereditary—if it was something that I inherited or if my own experiences led to depression. While I've argued the latter throughout the book, it's important to note that your family history plays a part as well. Think about it: why is it that they ask you about your family history when you go to a doctor's appointment? They're looking for possible matches that could help them treat you. Thus, the following conversation will help us understand that this thing called depression didn't just start with you. So, let yourself off the hook, and let's dive into it.

In Mark Wolynn's book "It Didn't Start with You," he talks about how inherited family trauma shapes who we are, yet how we can end the cycle.

During a traumatic incident, our thought processes can be scattered and disorganized in a way that we no longer recognize the memories belonging to the original event. Instead, fragments of memory, dispersed as images, body sensations, and words are stored in our unconscious and can become activated later by anything even remotely reminiscent of the original experience. Once they are triggered, it is as if an invisible rewind button has been pressed, causing us to reenact aspects of the original trauma in our day-to-day lives. Unconsciously, we could find ourselves reacting to certain people, events, or situations in old, familiar ways that echo the past.

This is interesting because my battle with depression and the PTSD diagnosis supports this argument. One of the things I relived day-to-day was the fear of loss. After losing Manon, I viewed my life through the lens of loss. I believed that the only way to experience life was to experience loss. Hence, why losing my wife didn't seem like such the big deal as it was. To lose something so dear and special was a part of life, because I had constantly loss so much before.

In my quest to figure out how to beat depression, I enlisted *repetitious compulsion,* a term coined by Sigmund Freud, as "an attempt of the unconscious to replay what's unresolved," so I could get it right. As Wolynn continues this conversation on family trauma, he argues this final point: "this unconscious drive to relive past events could be one of the mechanisms at work when families repeat unresolved traumas in future generations." And I believed that if I knew how I got to this point, I would be able to solve it. Having this logic is what caused the discontentment with my therapist. I didn't think they could get to the root of my issues, because it was locked up in my unconscious. The only person who could unravel this was me. This was very unhealthy thinking, but this is what it was. I wasn't sure how family trauma played a role in this, but it did.

According to Wolynn,

The latest research affirms that traumatic experience is passed on to future generations and that this emotional inheritance, hidden in everything from our gene expression to everyday language, plays a far greater role in our health than ever previously understood. Let's deal with emotional inheritance for a second.

Research affirms that our emotional inheritance is as determining as it is intransigent and imposing. Sometimes we make the mistake of thinking that our story started when we cried for the first time. Thinking this is a mistake because, just as we're the fruit of the union of an egg and a spermatozoon, we are also the product of a mixture. A mixture of desires, fantasies, fears and whole constellation of emotions and perceptions. If the stories of each members of a family are observed, you'll find essential coincidences and common axes. It would seem as if each individual were a chapter in a bigger story, which was written over different generations.

The process of transgenerational transmission is unconscious. Usually there are hidden or confusing situations, which generate embarrassment or fear. The descendants of someone who has suffered an untreated trauma bear the weight of that lack of resolution. They feel the presence of "something weird" which gravitates like a weight, but can't quite be defined.

For example: one of the major themes I see in my family is insecurity. I notice how many of us feel devalued or unloved. However, on the surface, you see a loving, caring, and embracing family. It would be quite difficult to enter into my family's presence and not feel like you are a part of the family.

Nevertheless, if you pulled us to the side and had one-on-ones, you would discover a lot of symptoms that would lead to depression. You would see how drugs and alcohol have led to emotional trauma amongst siblings. You would see classicism as it relates to the very well-educated, and slightly educated and how that breeds jealousy. There are a host of other issues, but I believe this has been the greatest challenge to our family: not understanding our value. And I believe this was an inherited trait.

Let me be clear, this was not a spoken trait or something we recited; it is strictly something we lived out through our actions, etc. And if you've paid attention up to this point, you will notice my greatest pain was my lack of understanding my value. *Does God really love? Will my job understand who I am, and pay me for it? Why am I such a threat? Does my wife get me?* All of these are my issues and my own insecurities that were inherited traits passed down from generation to generation. This emotional inheritance can manifest itself as an illness.

French psychoanalyst Francoise Dolto affirms:

The first generation is silent; the second generation carries it within their body. Just like a "collective unconscious" is a recognized thing, there is also a "family unconscious". Within this unconscious reside all of those silenced experiences. Experiences which have somehow been silenced, because they constitute a taboo. These may include suicides, abortions, mental illnesses, murders, bankruptcies, abuse, etc.

What I've realized as I battled with depression is this: I'm not only living my truth, but I'm also living a family truth. And this truth, if not acknowledged, will continue to be repeated.

Surviving Unmet Expectations

Over the past four chapters, we have discussed PTSD, job security, marriage, and a host of other areas that led to my depression, yet a more pressing question is: *how have I been able to survive unmet expectations?* I will detail a few actions that have helped me, and hopefully you can gain some insights and strategies that will help you as well.

Before I begin, let me express something that's critical to this conversation: I never stopped working, never stopped posting on social media, and I never stopped living. I suffered with depression *silently*. To this day, many reading this are surprised to know. So, let's talk strategy.

Mentorship Matters

I think it's vitally important to have a mentor…several mentors. Mentorship is vital to life and you need them. I talked about my pastor in part three, and despite letting him down, *he never let me down*. He, along with others, kept me afloat. Here are a few reasons why mentorship matters:

1. <u>You will be forced to talk.</u> Having someone who is dedicated to asking you the right questions and demanding real answers will help. My pastor always asked me "the why." Asking "the why" made me uncomfortable, because it forced me to live my truth. I had to sit with my truth and discover things about myself that I was afraid to confront. Having mentorship made me communicate. While, I still struggled at home, I was winning at work. This was semi-healthy, because I needed something to keep me going, and work helped.

2. <u>You will learn new skills.</u> Not only did I communicate my feelings better, I learned to be vulnerable. Yes, vulnerability to me is a skill. For years, I hid my truth, but I began to communicate more even if that made

others around me more uncomfortable with my thoughts. Having one-on-ones with my mentor made it easier for me when it came to sharing with my wife and therapist. Learning to be vulnerable allowed me to be free without judgement.

3. <u>Your work environment will change.</u> You will either embrace where you are, or you will move to a fitting space. I mentioned in part three about tension with a former supervisor. My pastor changed our organizational chart, and made the environment more collaborative. My former supervisor and I are just fine now. We work as a team. I'm also compensated well. I have benefits, and I feel like a valuable member of the team. While my situation is vastly different from many—meaning your mentor may not be your boss—having someone who has insight with career placement and purpose will help a great deal. I always communicate with my mentor about where I see myself. Thus, making it easier for him to lend advice and assist me in those areas. Communicate where you want to go, and allow your mentor to guide. This will help a lot.

4. <u>Mentors are disciplinarians that create necessary boundaries that we cannot set for ourselves.</u> As I was drifting far away from myself, my mentor always reminded me of where I needed to be. I must admit, I didn't listen, and it cost me a lot, but he never stopped believing in me.

5. <u>Mentors can be connectors.</u> Playing a dual role of teacher and connector, a mentor can provide access to those within your industry that are willing to invest in your company. They offer their skills and expertise, introduce you to talent that can fuel your business and help you get closer to your target audience. My mentor willingly shared his network with me by taking me to events and making introductions that led to many opportunities I would not have otherwise had. This was

probably the most critical thing for me. I continue to thrive and find opportunities because of my mentor's connections. Everything I've wanted, I've received.

I'm alive today because I have a mentor that cares. I have several individuals who mentor me, and I am grateful for them all. This has been a critical part of my journey to recovery.

Counseling Matters

It's been ten years since my first counseling session, and I can honestly say counseling works if you do the work. I'm now doing something called *emotional therapy*-- a short-term form of <u>therapy </u>that focuses on adult relationships and <u>attachment</u>/bonding. The therapist and clients look at patterns in the relationship and take steps to create a more secure bond and develop more trust to move the relationship in a healthier, more positive direction. I am grateful for this type of therapy. My ex-wife became aware this model of therapy first and eventually shared it with me. She even went as far to find the perfect therapist for me. Even in pain and brokenness, she's still been there for me, and I'm grateful. Let's talk more about emotional therapy for a moment.

According to *Psychology Today*, here's what you can expect with therapy,

An EFT (Emotional Focused Therapist) observes the dynamics between clients in the therapy setting, ties this behavior to the dynamics in their home lives, and helps direct new conversations and interactions based on more honest feelings. To accomplish this, your therapist will encourage you to look at your current emotional issues and then help you discover feelings and emotions that you may not realize you have. You may discover deeper past feelings and vulnerabilities that are blocked by the more immediate emotions you display in your current relationship. You will learn to express these emotions in a way that will help you connect, rather than disconnect with your partner or family member. You will learn new ways to listen and stay attuned to another's emotions and discover more productive ways to respond to emotional situations.

How It Works

EFT focuses on the present time to makes changes in the here and now. There are three steps, or stages, of EFT. The first is to de-escalate the couple's or family member's negative cycle of interactions, and help them see and understand what is happening in their relationship. Clients come to see that the problems lie in insecurities and distance. The next stage is to restructure interactions, wherein the therapist helps clients discuss their fears in the relationship, using language that doesn't push the other away. Clients learn to turn toward each other and discuss their needs and they become more open and responsive to each other. Consolidation is the third stage of EFT, wherein the therapist helps clients see how they got into negative patterns and points out how they were able to change those patterns and can continue these types of conversations in the future.

What to Look for in an Emotionally Focused Therapist

An EFT therapist is a licensed mental <u>health</u> professional who has additional training and experience in EFT. The International Centre for Excellence in Emotionally Focused Therapy works with affiliated EFT communities around the world to provide certification. In addition to checking credentials, it is important to find an EFT therapist with whom you feel comfortable working.

This has been really beneficial for me. We focus on emotional stability and we talk about the expectations I've levied against myself and debunk them. I have a lot of unmet expectations, and I often blame myself for not achieving them. But in emotional therapy, I'm free of those things. I blamed myself for not honoring my vows, and loving my wife as she needed, however, in emotional therapy, we accept it and embrace it, but we don't stay there—we find peace and healing. It works, and I believe in it.

Self-Discovery Matters

One of my greatest challenges has been reconnecting with self. After losing my best friend, I became nonchalant, very mild mannered, and carefree. A lot of the things that once mattered no longer mattered. I really didn't care about career moves, nor did I value family as I should have. I was living an internally isolated life, while portraying to the world an image that wasn't true. Again, I'd 'catfished' myself, and only I knew it.

What has helped me, however, are these five practical principles below:

1. *I schedule "me" time.* I devote myself to doing things that matter to me. I love sports. Thus, I have season tickets to the Atlanta Falcons games, and I always make time to watch LeBron James play. These things make me happy. I have learned that only you can make you happy. People and things can add to your happiness, but you're responsible for your own happiness. I love coffee as well, so I spend time searching out the best coffee houses in every city I visit, and I spend countless hours there doing work, and drinking great coffee. Finally, I travel quite a bit--mainly for work and slightly for leisure. I think it's important to do the things that make you feel most alive, and that's what I'm doing.

2. *I journal.* Along with therapy, I journal daily. Anytime I feel low, I write down those emotions in my iPhone and why I'm feeling them. I heard it said once, *finding time to journal simply means taking the time to get in touch with your real emotions.* These are the emotions we often repress or ignore as we work, pick up the kids, and handle other responsibilities. I write down why I'm worried, what I can control, and what I can't. I write

why I'm grateful, and all of the things that made me
happy for that day.

3. *I pray often.* One of the greatest threats to my marriage
and purpose was that I removed prayer from being a
priority. I no longer believed that it worked.
Communing with God didn't seem real anymore, and
boy was I wrong. Hear me people: *PRAYER WORKS.* I
pray every day, and I believe in the power of prayer. I
know without a doubt, that I'm still alive because
someone prayed for me when I couldn't pray for myself.
As the late James Cone stated, "when we pray, our souls
are laid before God." My soul is constantly before God,
and it's helping me recover.

4. *Forgiveness has been very essential to my quest for
wholeness.* Mark Twain says, "Forgiveness is the
fragrance that the violet sheds on the heel that has
crushed it." I was awful towards my ex-wife. I hurt
others along my journey as well. I disconnected from
friends and those who really cared about me. Yet,
somehow, all of them have forgiven me. I'm so grateful
for this, however, I am struggling to forgive myself. It's
a process, but I have started the process. I think it's
important to accept your part in any mistakes, but don't
beat yourself up as I have. It's easier said than done, but
it's possible to forgive yourself once you admit what
you've done to cause the brokenness.

5. *I have reconnected with friends.* I went back to my old
neighborhood where I grew up, and began new
friendships with old friends. I'm assisting one of my
friends with coaching our neighborhood baseball team.
Being around my friends has started to remind me of
who I was. The fun, exciting, and joking guy. In
addition, I've made new friends, and it's wonderful. I
feel alive and free. I'm not hiding behind an image or
something fake. The people who love me--really love

me. Stay connected to those who want the connection, and release those who don't. It's simple.

Now What?

You all have explored a lot. I allowed you guys to tap in and experience portions of my world. Of course, I didn't reveal everything, but I shared the things that led to my depression.

I must admit. I am nervous, yet excited about releasing this story. I didn't want to let anyone into my space, but I realized so many millennials and others are silently suffering with depression and few people understand.

I was low, and almost quit on life, but grace and a detour sign saved my life. Every day is a journey, and my quest for wholeness and healing is incomplete. I strive daily to be intentional about creating happiness, and not falling into deep darkness. It's not easy. It's hard. but I'm going to continue to do the work and you should too.

For what I know is this: "the race is not given to given to the swift or the strong, but to the one who endures to the end"-Ecclesiastes 9:11.

References

1. https://www.psychologytoday.com/us/therapy-types/emotionally-focused-therapy

2. https://fightthenewdrug.org/porn-can-make-you-more-depressed-and-lonely/

3. https://www.huffingtonpost.com/wray-herbert/choosing-sadness-the-iron_b_7024348.html

4. http://www.hopexchange.com/Statistics.htm

5. https://www.webmd.com/depression/features/divorcing-depression#4

6. http://thriveworks.com/blog/stigma-with-counseling-in-the-black-community/

7. http://kimeisenberg.com/blog/career-strategy/this-is-a-post-about-depression-and-your-career/

8. https://www.forbes.com/sites/danschawbel/2013/05/28/cy-wakeman-how-to-evaluate-the-roi-of-an-employee/#2b8ca1cb7c3e

9. https://www.urbandictionary.com/define.php?term=hater

10. https://www.verywellmind.com/emotional-needs-not-filled-marriage-partner-2303305

11. https://www.forbes.com/sites/lizryan/2017/03/01/ten-signs-your-boss-secs-you-as-a-threat/#47cb74376071

12. *https://www.forbes.com/sites/karlmoore/2014/10/02/mil lennials-work-for-purpose-not-paycheck/#5c58edaf6a51*

13. *http://www.youngadultmoney.com/2016/09/14/simple-millennials-want-more-money/*

14. https://www.gotquestions.org/armor-bearer.html

15. https://exploringyourmind.com/emotional-inheritance-ancestors

16. https://www.healthyplace.com/blogs/copingwithdepress ion/2017/09/friendships-and-depression/

17. http://news.gallup.com/poll/191462/gallup-analysis-millennials-marriage-family.aspx

18. file:///Users/dacarimiddlebrooks/Downloads/Shifting_ Work_and_Family_Trends_among_Millennials_P0cSG HW.pdf

19. http://time.com/4748357/milennials-values-census-report/

20. http://www.pewresearch.org/fact-tank/2016/01/08/qa-why-millennials-are-less-religious-than-older-americans/

21. https://www.forbes.com/sites/williamarruda/2017/08/02 /the-surprising-thing-millennials-want-from-their-career/#60f9ceea24fc

22. Chris Hayes book: Twilight of Elites

23. https://www.today.com/news/born-between-1981-1996-
you-re-millennial-now-according-pew-t124232

24. https://www.forbes.com/sites/carolinebeaton/2016/03/2
9/the-too-many-passions-problem-4-things-you-can-do-
today-to-choose-your-perfect-career/#7b316a1829af

25. https://addicted2success.com/success-advice/16-
reasons-why-its-important-to-follow-your-dreams/

26. https://dhproject.org/symptoms-of-
ptsd/?utm_source=5SMGoogle&utm_medium=CPC&ut
m_campaign=PTSD&gclid=EAIaIQobChMIkqHJnaqD
2gIVi2p-Ch0T2Q39EAAYAiAAEgJm-PD_BwE

27. Baumeister, R. F., & Leary, M. R. (1995). The need to
belong: Desire for interpersonal attachments as a
fundamental human motivation. Psychological Bulletin,
117(3), 497-529. doi:10.1037/0033-2909.117.3.497

28. Cohen, S. (2004). Social relationships and health.
American Psychologist, 59(8), 676-684

29. Diener, E., & Seligman, M. E. (2002). Very happy
people. Psychological Science, 13(1), 81-84.
doi:10.1111/1467- 9280.00415

30. Larson, R., Mannell, R., & Zuzanek, J. (1986). Daily
well-being of older adults with friends and family.
Psychology and Aging, 1(2), 117-126.
doi:10.1037/0882-7974.1.2.117

31. Thoits, P. A. (1995). Stress, coping, and social support
processes: Where are we? What next? Journal of Health
and Social Behavior, 35, 53-79. doi:10.2307/2626957

32. https://repository.upenn.edu/cgi/viewcontent.cgi?article
=1019&context=mcnair_scholars

33. https://ochen.com/transcript-of-simon-sineks-millennials-in-the-workplace-interview

34. https://www.psychologytoday.com/us/blog/dream-factory/201603/nightmares-after-trauma

35. https://www.psychologytoday.com/us/blog/emotional-fitness/201108/10-ways-make-and-be-great-friend

Made in the USA
Columbia, SC
05 June 2018